LIBRARY

OF THE

# POETS LAUREATE

# VERSES

## OF THE

# POETS LAUREATE

### FROM JOHN DRYDEN TO ANDREW MOTION

COLLECTED BY
## HILARY LAURIE

INTRODUCED BY
## ANDREW MOTION

TED SMART

# ACKNOWLEDGEMENTS

## ILLUSTRATIONS

PP.16, 28, 38, 43, 46, 52, 62, 65, 76, 124, 133, 145, 169
HULTON GETTY PICTURE COLLECTION;

P.182 FAY GODWIN / CAMERA PRESS;

P.196 WILLIAM TEAKLE / FABER;

THE DEVICE USED ON THE TITLE-PAGE AND
ELSEWHERE IN THIS BOOK IS BY WILLIAM HOGARTH.

## TEXTS

THE SOCIETY OF AUTHORS AS THE LITERARY
REPRESENTATIVE OF THE ESTATE OF JOHN MASEFIELD;

REPRINTED FROM "POETICAL WORKS OF ROBERT BRIDGES"
(1936) BY PERMISSION OF OXFORD UNIVERSITY PRESS;

"THE COMPLETE POEMS" BY C. DAY LEWIS, PUBLISHED
BY SINCLAIR-STEVENSON (1992), COPYRIGHT © 1992
IN THIS EDITION, AND THE ESTATE OF C DAY LEWIS;

SLOUGH, IN WESTMINSTER ABBBEY, A SHROPSHIRE LAD,
IN A BATH TEASHOP, SUN AND FUN, HOW TO GET ON
IN SOCIETY, LATE FLOWERING LUST BY JOHN BETJEMAN,
PUBLISHED BY JOHN MURRAY (PUBLISHERS) LTD;

THE THOUGHT-FOX FROM "THE HAWK IN THE RAIN";
FERN AND PIBROCH FROM "WODWO"; CROW'S FALL,
CROW'S VANITY, CONJURING IN HEAVEN FROM "CROW";
A MARCH CALF FROM "SEASON SONGS"; DAFFODILS
FROM "BIRTHDAY LETTERS"; LITTLE SALMON HYMN
FROM "RAIN-CHARM FOR THE DUCHY AND OTHER
LAUREATE POEMS" BY TED HUGHES, REPRINTED WITH
PERMISSION FROM FABER AND FABER;

IN THE ATTIC, A BLOW TO THE HEAD, ON THE TABLE, HEY
NONNY FROM "SELECTED POEMS 1976-1997" BY ANDREW
MOTION, REPRINTED WITH PERMISSION FROM FABER
AND FABER; EPITHALAMIUM © 1999 ANDREW MOTION.

# TABLE OF CONTENTS

# Introduction

WHAT does it mean to be Poet Laureate? Is it an honour, or a job, or both? Are you commissioned by others or yourself? Do you hold up a mirror to the state and to monarchy, or are you free to comment and even criticise? Are its various pressures enabling or crushing?

This book is much more likely to provoke such questions than resolve them. Given the different degrees of significance attached to the post in the past, and the mixed abilities of those who have filled the position, the selection is bound to be a rag-bag. A rag-bag that, even before it is examined, stands a chance of being condemned as second-rate.

Why? Because a good many Poets Laureate have used their period of office to produce work that is merely sentimental or sycophantic. Because others have been appointed at such a late date in their careers, it has proved impossible for them to write as well as they once might have done. Because others again were simply the wrong choice—or, at least, chosen for the wrong, subservient reasons.

Faced with such a catalogue, any fair-minded person will want to point out exceptions proving the rule. They could do worse than begin at a tangent, and say that while some Laureates have focused entirely on writing, others have combined it with doing. John Betjeman, for instance, though ill for much of his time in office, went on developing his TV personality in order to promote the taste by which he wished to be judged. And Ted Hughes continued the work he had begun in his pre-Laureate days—work for poetry in translation and for the Arvon Foundation.

Then again, some Laureates have interpreted their writing-role so broadly, they have been able to spread the burden of their responsibilities, and shoulder them comparatively easily.    Two poets stand out in this respect : John Dryden and Alfred, Lord Tennyson.    Even though Dryden was appointed as the (first) Laureate for his lines defending Charles II, and even though he worked closely with the king to rhyme the confusion of their enemies, his skill in combining the quotidian with the ceremonial means that a human warmth still glows in his best performances. In his "Song for St. Cecilia's Day, 1687" for example :

> The Trumpet's loud clangour
> Excites us to Arms
> With shrill Notes of Anger
> And mortal Alarms.
> The double double double beat
> Of the thundering Drum
> Cryes, heark the Foes come ;
> Charge, Charge, 'tis too late to retreat.

It's the skittish realism of "double double double" here, and its syncopated ripple, that gives these lines their special suppleness and charm.    They prove that Dryden's auditory imagination is working independently of his merely rational intelligence.    They are at once respectful of the occasion he has been commissioned to honour, and able to transfigure it.

The same is true of Tennyson's most successful Laureate

poems—"The Charge of the Light Brigade", or the even more impressive "Ode on the Death of the Duke of Wellington". The tone in both of these is more sombre than in Dryden's "Song", and there is a thick overlay of heroic and neo-classical reference. But there is also a powerful sense of the particular within the universal, of the men inside the uniforms :

> Under the cross of gold
> That shines over city and river,
> There shall he rest for ever
> Among the wise and the bold.
> Let the bell be tolled :
> And a reverent people behold
> The towering car, the sable steeds :
> Bright let it be with blazoned deeds,
> Dark in its funeral fold.

Dryden and Tennyson are a welcome counter-weight to Laureates such as Laurence Eusden, Colley Cibber, William Whitehead and Henry Pye. But their power is supported by a (possibly surprising) number of other distinguished poems in this book : modest but memorable lyrics by John Masefield, and heroic grapplings by Hughes. Where most of Hughes's predecessors had concentrated on the surface-realities of a particular moment, he dived beneath the appearance of things, looking for fundamental symbolic values. The result is a body of Laureate work that puzzled or even irritated some of its first readers, but which, as time passes, we can see making very strong, fascinating and primitive connections between monarchy, the country, and poetry itself.

In other words, this anthology is partly of interest for the work that it contains, and partly because it allows us to watch a gradually unfolding argument about national character, and about the form and role of public poetry. Three hundred years after the first of our nineteen Poets Laureate was appointed, it is no longer possible or desirable to speak for a centred and simplified version of the "nation", as Tennyson's "Ode" does. Neither is it possible or desirable for a Poet Laureate to treat a Royal subject as being somehow super-human. Indeed, if the post of Laureate is to survive in any meaningful way, within our diverse culture and diffused society, it will require a complex negotiation between the individuals involved and their wider world, between private and public, between tradition and the present.

The need for these realignments helps to explain why there was so much fuss in the press when Hughes died, and then again when I was appointed as his successor. Even though most people's attention was directed towards personalities, rather than poetry, the sound of a different conversation could be heard in the background : a conversation about cohesion (or the lack of it), and about the unlikelihood of any one poet being able to speak for everyone.

There were other considerations, too, that greatly intensified the argument. During the fifteen-odd years that Hughes had been Laureate, the Royal family itself had been through unprecedented changes. How could a Laureate hope to write with traditional bell-ringing, confetti-throwing confidence about a Royal wedding, say, since the previous several had ended in disaster ? Or again, how could the ranks of younger contemporary poets—whose image had been so much altered and lifted during the 1980s—easily open to admit a new Laureate, unless that person was pretty obviously "one of them"?

No two poets could have reacted to these challenges in the same way. My own response has been to divide (in my mind's eye) the post of Poet Laureate into two parts: a doing part and a writing part. The doing part has very little clear precedent, as I've already indicated: some Laureates have performed a good many public works, others very few. My own plans include: the establishment of several Writers' Houses around the country, where poets (and others) who are not able to find quiet time at home can concentrate on a particular piece of work; the promotion of poetry in schools—by encouraging its reading and writing where too little exists, and supporting the many committed teachers who might need refreshing; the soliciting and editing of a regular series of anthologies that will contain poems about national issues—by unknown as well as well-known poets; the redefinition of the Queen's Gold Medal for Poetry, and an annual radio-lecture by the winner, who would also be invited to introduce a programme of work by younger writers.

These and other such schemes will be designed to endorse the whole range of poetry being written in these islands, rather than privilege one kind in particular. Like everyone else, I have my special tastes and preferences, and my own ideas about what works and what doesn't. But as Laureate I think the important thing is to work for everyone to have their equal opportunity, so they can find their ideal audience. So that poetry can become a part of our national conversation in a way that is at once relaxed and urgent.

The writing part of the position is much more clearly defined by tradition—the tradition represented in this book. Though as I've also indicated, this tradition now looks as though it has reached a watershed. It is difficult for me to anticipate how I'll deal with this—for the simple reason that even commissioned poems do not obey clear rules of supply and demand. They will (they should, if they are true poems) always have an unpredictable and unpredicted element—like "double double double".

All the same, I can identify some of the principles I hold dear. I intend to honour my (informal) obligation to write poems for notable Royal occasions, but to make them part of a larger pattern of poems about national, civic and political issues. I cannot, however, imagine writing any of these poems in a voice that is significantly unlike the one I normally use. Although I am a political animal, and have been a member of the Labour Party for many years, I have never felt able—and have not wanted—to address public issues in any head-on way. Like Keats, I "hate poetry that has a palpable design on us", and also like Keats I've always felt that "axioms in philosophy are not axioms until they are proved upon our pulses". Readers are more likely to take a point in a poem, and to feel persuaded by it, if that point achieves its direction indirectly. If it is sensuous and dramatic, rather than mechanical and merely assertive.

Following Hughes's death, an American newspaper described the post of Poet Laureate as "a double-edged chalice". It is— for all the reasons given here. At the end of the twentieth century, it distils a number of potent and large anxieties : about government, about identity, and about the value and use of art.

But it also offers wonderful chances : to promote the whole community of poets, to reaffirm the primitive connections that poetry can make between people and their feeling, and to adapt traditional ways of speaking and commemorating to make them more human. Which not only means more approachable, but also more realistic—eager to "speak truth to power", as Hazlitt put it, rather than speak on behalf of power.

*Andrew Motion*
London, 1999

Mr. John Dryden

# JOHN DRYDEN

1631–1700

John Dryden was the first official poet laureate, appointed by Charles II in 1668. He was the ideal man for the job—the best poet, dramatist, translator and critic of the age, the first truly all-round man of English letters.

All his life he was close to the centre of political power, which was constantly changing. When Charles I was beheaded in 1649 the monarchy gave way to the Commonwealth. The Stuart kings returned in 1660 only to be replaced by William III in 1689. Like many of his contemporaries, Dryden feared a total collapse of law and order. He was ready to support a strong leader even if this meant changing political or religious allegiance. So he would write "Heroic Stanzas" on the death of Cromwell, and "Annus Mirabilis" in defence of the new King Charles II. His reward was the laureateship. There were no obligations attached to the appointment, but he was promised £100 per year and "one butt or Pype of the best Canary Wyne".

Dryden's greatest service as laureate lay in his satires, in which he acted as both advocate and spokesman for the King and his interests. At this time the court was much closer to the heart of political controversy than it is now. Stories are told of Dryden strolling in the Mall with the King discussing what the poet might write next to harm His Majesty's enemies. It is hard now to recapture the power of his poems because they are concerned with historical events rather than individual experience. His great satire "Absalom and Achitophel" addresses the Popish Plot ; "MacFlecknoe" is a battle of wits with the dramatist Thomas Shadwell who would succeed him as poet laureate. Dryden's translation of Virgil is one of the great master-pieces of translation in English.

But many of his maxims and observations endure, for, as T. S. Eliot remarked, he had the ability "to make the small into the great, the prosaic into the poetic, the trivial into the magnificent". He brought an authority to the laureateship which few of his successors have matched. Yet he has been the only holder of the office to be sacked. When the Protestant William III came to the throne in 1689 he required all holders of high office to take an oath of allegiance. This Dryden, now a Catholic, refused to do and his appointment was not renewed. He returned to writing for the theatre and to his translations until his death some ten years later.

## Why should a foolish marriage vow
*from* Marriage à-la-Mode

*This is a song from one of Dryden's best-known comedies.*

Why should a foolish marriage vow,
    Which long ago was made,
Oblige us to each other now
    When passion is decayed ?
We loved and we loved as long as we could,
    Till our love was loved out in us both :
But our marriage is dead when the pleasure is fled :
    'Twas pleasure first made it an oath.

If I have pleasures for a friend,
    And farther love in store,
What wrong has he whose joys did end,
    And who could give no more ?
'Tis a madness that he should be jealous of me,
    Or that I should bar him of another ;
For all we can gain is to give ourselves pain,
    When neither can hinder the other.

## *from* Astrea Redux

*Dryden wrote this in 1660 to welcome the Restoration of the monarchy, and the return of Charles II, after the death of Oliver Cromwell.*

And welcome now (*Great Monarch*) to your own ;
Behold th' approaching cliffes of *Albion* ;
It is no longer Motion cheats your view,
As you meet it, the Land approacheth you.
The Land returns, and in the white it wears
The marks of penitence and sorrow bears.
But you, whose goodness your discent doth show,
Your Heav'nly Parentage and earthly too ;
By that same mildness which your Fathers Crown
Before did ravish, shall secure your own.
Not ty'd to rules of Policy, you find
Revenge less sweet than a forgiving mind.
Thus when th' Almighty would to *Moses* give
A sight of all he could behold and live ;
A voice before his entry did proclaim
*Long-Suff'ring, Goodness, Mercy* in his Name.

Your Pow'r to Justice doth submit your Cause,
Your Goodness only is above the Laws ;
Whose rigid letter while pronounc'd by you
Is softer made.  So winds that tempests brew
When through *Arabian* Groves they take their flight
Made wanton with rich Odours, lose their spight.
And as those Lees that trouble it, refine
The agitated Soul of Generous Wine,

So tears of joy for your returning spilt,
Work out and expiate our former guilt.
Methinks I see those Crowds on *Dovers* Strand
Who in their hast to welcome you to Land
Choak'd up the Beach with their still growing store,
And made a wilder Torrent on the shore.
While spurr'd with eager thoughts of past delight
Those who had seen you, court a second sight;
Preventing still your steps, and making hast
To meet you often where so e're you past.
How shall I speak of that triumphant Day
When you renew'd the expiring Pomp of *May!*
(A month that owns an Intrest in your Name:
You and the Flow'rs are its peculiar Claim.)
That Star that at your Birth shone out so bright
It stain'd the duller Suns Meridian light,
Did once again its potent Fires renew
Guiding our eyes to find and worship you.

## Death, the End of All

*From Dryden's translation of* On the Nature of Things *by the Roman poet and philosopher Lucretius.*

What has this bugbear death to frighten man,
If souls can die, as well as bodies can?
For, as before our birth we felt no pain,
When Punic arms infested land and main,

When heaven and earth were in confusion hurled
For the debated empire of the world,
Which awed with dreadful expectation lay,
Sure to be slaves uncertain who should sway :
So, when our mortal frame shall be disjoined,
The lifeless lump uncoupled from the mind,
From sense of grief and pain we shall be free ;
We shall not feel, because we shall not *be*.
Though earth in seas, and seas in heaven were lost,
We should not move, we only should be tossed.
    Nay, ev'n suppose when we have suffered fate,
The soul could feel in her divided state,
What's that to us ?  for we are only we
While souls and bodies in one frame agree.
Nay, though our atoms should revolve by chance,
And matter leap into the former dance ;
Though time our life and motion could restore,
And make our bodies what they were before,
What gain to us would all this bustle bring ?
The new-made man would be another thing ;
When once an interrupting pause is made,
That individual being is decayed.
We, who are dead and gone, shall bear no part
In all the pleasures, nor shall feel the smart,
Which to that other mortal shall accrue,
Whom of our matter time shall mould anew.
    For backward if you look on that long space
Of ages past, and view the changing face

Of matter, tossed and variously combined
In sundry shapes, 'tis easy for the mind
From thence t' infer that seeds of things have been
In the same order as they now are seen ;
Which yet our dark remembrance cannot trace,
Because a pause of life, a gaping space
Has come betwixt, where memory lies dead
And all the wandering motions from the sense are fled.
For whoso'er shall in misfortunes live,
Must *be* when those misfortunes shall arrive ;
And since the man who *is* not, feels not woe
(For death exempts him, and wards off the blow,
Which we the living only feel and bear),
What is there left for us in death to fear ?
When once that pause of life has come between,
'Tis just the same as we had never been.


## A Song for St. Cecilia's Day, 1687

*This was performed, to music, on 22 November 1687, at the annual celebrations in Stationers' Hall which marked the feast day of St. Cecilia, patron saint of music.*

From harmony, from heavenly harmony,
This universal frame began :
When Nature underneath a heap
Of jarring atoms lay.
And could not heave her head,

The tuneful voice was heard from high,
   "Arise, ye more than dead !"
Then cold and hot and moist and dry
In order to their stations leap,
   And music's power obey.
From harmony, from heavenly harmony.
   This universal frame began :
   From harmony to harmony
Through all the compass of the notes it ran,
The diapason closing full in man.

   What passion cannot music raise and quell ?
   When Jubal struck and chorded shell,
   His listening brethren stood around,
   And wondering on their faces fell
   To worship that celestial sound.
Less than a god they thought there could not dwell
   Within the hollow of that shell,
   That spoke so sweetly and so well
What passion cannot music raise and quell ?

   The trumpet's loud clangour
      Excites us to arms,
   With shrill notes of anger
      And mortal alarms.
   The double, double, double beat
      Of the thundering drum
   Cries, "Hark !  the foes come ;
      Charge, charge, 'tis too late to retreat !"

The soft complaining flute
In dying notes discovers
The woes of hopeless lovers,
Whose dirge is whispered by the warbling lute.

Sharp violins proclaim
Their jealous pangs and desperation,
Fury, frantic indignation,
Depth of pains, and height of passion
For the fair, disdainful dame.

But oh ! what art can teach,
What human voice can reach
The sacred organ's praise ?
Notes inspiring holy love,
Notes that wing their heavenly ways
To mend the choirs above.

Orpheus could lead the savage race,
And trees unrooted left their place,
Sequacious of the lyre :
But bright Cecilia raised the wonder higher :
When to her organ vocal breath was given
An angel heard, and straight appeared.
Mistaking earth for heaven.

## GRAND CHORUS

*As from the power of sacred lays*
*The spheres began to move,*
*And sung the great Creator's praise*
*To all the blessed above ;*
*So when the last and dreadful hour*
*This crumbling pageant shall devour,*
*The trumpet shall be heard on high,*
*The dead shall live, the living die,*
*And music shall untune the sky.*

# The nocturnal activities of Messalina, wife of the Emperor Claudius
### *a translation from* The Sixth Satire of Juvenal

The good old sluggard but began to snore,
When from his side up rose th' imperial whore ;
She who preferred the pleasures of the night
To pomps, that are but impotent delight,
Strode from the palace with an eager pace,
To cope with a more masculine embrace.
Muffled she marched, like Juno in a cloud,
Of all her train but one poor wench allowed ;
One whom in secret service she could trust :
The rival and companion of her lust.

To the known brothel-house she takes her way,
And for a nasty room gives double pay ;
That room in which the rankest harlot lay.
Prepared for fight, expectingly she lies,
With heaving breasts and with desiring eyes.
Still as one drops, another takes his place,
And baffled still succeeds to like disgrace.
At length, when friendly darkness is expired,
And every strumpet from her cell retired,
She lags behind and, lingering at the gate,
With a repining sigh submits to fate ;
All filth without, and all afire within,
Tired with the toil, unsated with the sin.
Old Caesar's bed the modest matron seeks,
The steam of lamps still hanging on her cheeks
In ropy smut ; thus foul, and thus bedight,
She brings him back the product of the night.

# THOMAS SHADWELL

1642–1692

Dryden cannot have approved of the choice of Thomas Shadwell to succeed him. The two men had once been friends but, after a very public falling out, each fiercely attacked the other in print. Dryden ridiculed Shadwell's habit of taking opium, his heavy drinking and his ignorance of the classics. In his satirical poem "MacFlecknoe" he claimed,

> The rest to some faint meaning make pretence,
> But Shadwell never deviates into sense.

Shadwell fought back, calling Dryden "an abandoned rascal", "half wit, half fool", but he was outmatched.

Shadwell did not place much importance on the laureateship. His poetry was so without significance that the editors of his collected works chose not to include any of it. He was much more successful as a dramatist and several of his comedies were greatly admired. He was poet laureate for only four years, but during this time he dutifully produced a yearly ode on the sovereign's birthday, and he began the custom, which lasted over 100 years, of writing an ode to mark the New Year. Invariably these odes were mechanical and dull, although there were subjects and opportunities on hand for writers of heroic verse. William III could have been presented as a great liberator who had brought unhappy, difficult times to an end, but Shadwell never rose to the occasion, as, for instance, in his poem celebrating the King's return from Ireland after the Battle of the Boyne. At the start of the battle the King was hit by a cannon ball and it was rumoured that he had been killed. Instead, injured, he led his army to victory. His poet laureate could only remark:

But heaven of you took such peculiar care
That soon the Royal Breach it did repair.

Shadwell's death was sudden and unexpected, possibly due to an opium overdose. Previously he had expressed the curious wish to be buried in flannel. He has the misfortune to be remembered as the man Dryden so brilliantly mocked. And Dryden was not his only critic : Rochester, another contemporary poet and satirist, observed that if Shadwell "had burnt all he wrote, and printed all he spoke, he would have had more wit and humour than any other poet".

---

## *from* An Ode on the Queen's Birthday
Sung before their Majesties at Whitehall, by Tho. Shadwell

Now does the glorious Day appear,
The mightiest Day of all the Year,
Not anyone such joy could bring,
Not that which ushers in the Spring.
That of ensuing Plenty hopes does give,
This did the hope of Liberty retrieve ;
This does our Fertile Isle with Glory Crown,
And all the Fruits it yields we now can call our own.
On this blest day was our Restorer born,
Farr above all let this the Kalendar Adorn.
*Now, now with our united Voice*
*Let us aloud proclaim our Joys ;*
Io Triumphe *let us sing*
*And make Heav'ns mighty concave ring.*

# Song

*This charming song is unusually light-hearted for its period.*

Bright was the morning, cool the Air,
    Serene was all the Sky,
When on the waves I left my fair,
    The centre of my joy;
Heaven and Nature smiling were,
    And nothing sad but I.

Each rosy field its odour spread,
    All fragrant was the shore,
Each river God rose from his bed,
    And sigh'd and owned her power;
Curling their waves they deckt their head
    As proud of what they bore.

Glide on, ye waters, bear these lines
    And tell her how I am opprest;
Bear all my sighs, ye gentle winds;
    And waft them to her breast;
Tell her if ere she prove unkind
    I never shall have rest.

*There is no extant portrait of Nahum Tate.*

# Nahum Tate

1652–1715

Nahum Tate is remembered for three things, none of them to do with his laureateship : his work with Dryden on the second part of Dryden's satirical poem "Absalom and Achitophel" ; his revisions and adaptations of other men's plays, most memorably Shakespeare's *King Lear,* from which he removed so much of the tragedy that it had a happy ending ; and his metrical versions of the psalms, which have been admired and have lasted better than the majority of laureate poems.

Tate was born in Dublin, son of Dr. Faithful Teate, acting provost of Trinity College who lost his house when it was burned down by the rebels on whom he had informed. His son left Ireland for London and the life of a writer. He worked principally in the theatre, but he also produced a lot of occasional verse and translations, including one entitled "Syphilis : or, a Poetical History of the French Disease". He was poet laureate for twenty-three years, appointed on the death of Shadwell in 1692 by William and Mary, outliving them both and their successor, Queen Anne, and seeing in the first Hanoverian king, George I.

Tate was one of the most prolific poets laureate but he must be accounted one of the worst. His sycophantic, over-coloured poems have little to recommend them. He was mocked by his contemporaries, scorned by Swift and dismissed by Pope. He seems to have been an honest enough man—one of his friends described him as "a free good-natured fuddling companion", but he struggled hard to make ends meet. He died in miserable circumstances, hiding from his creditors in the Mint in Southwark. Literary historians can find little good to say of him, but churchgoers have reason to think more fondly of him.

# As pants the hart for cooling streams

*Tate's metrical versions of the psalms were, and still are, much admired.*

As pants the hart for cooling streams
    When heated in the chase,
So longs my soul, O God, for Thee,
    And Thy refreshing grace.

For Thee, my God, the living God,
    My thirsty soul doth pine :
O when shall I behold Thy face,
    Thou Majesty divine !

Why restless, why cast down, my soul ?
    Hope still, and thou shalt sing
The praise of Him Who is thy God,
    Thy health's eternal spring.

To Father, Son, and Holy Ghost,
    The God Whom we adore,
Be Glory, as it was, is now,
    And shall be evermore.

## The Round

*First published in Tate's* Collected Poems *in 1677.*

How vain a thing is Man whom toys delight,
　　And shadows fright !
Variety of impertinence
Might give our dotage some pretence ;
But to a circle bound
We toil in a dull round :
We sit, move, eat and drink,
We dress, undress, discourse and think
By the same passions hurried on,
Imposing, or imposed upon :
We pass the time in sport or toil,
We plough the seas, or safer soil :
Thus all that we project and do,
We did it many a year ago.
We travel still a beaten way,
And yet how eager rise we to pursue
Th' affairs of each returning day,
As if its entertainments were surprising all and new.

# While shepherds watched their flocks by night

*Tate's best-known piece of work, although few people could name him as its author.*

While shepherds watched their flocks by night,
    All seated on the ground,
The Angel of the Lord came down,
    And glory shone around.

"Fear not", said he ; for mighty dread
    Had seized their troubled mind ;
"Glad tidings of great joy I bring
    To you and all mankind.

"To you, in David's town, this day,
    Is born of David's line
A Saviour, Who is Christ the Lord ;
    And this shall be the sign :

"The heavenly Babe you there shall find
    To human view displayed,
All meanly wrapped in swathing bands,
    And in a manger laid."

Thus spake the seraph ; and forthwith
    Appeared a shining throng
Of Angels, praising God, who thus
    Addressed their joyful song :

"All glory be to God on high,
    And to the earth be peace,
Good-will, henceforth, from heaven to men
    Begin, and never cease."

## Mr. Tate, the Poet Laureat's Song, for His Majesty's Birthday,

### May the 28<sup>th</sup>, 1715

*This was written for King George I's birthday, which, in spite of Jacobite rioting and unrest, was celebrated with great brilliance.*

Arise, harmonious pow'rs
From your Elysian bow'rs
And Nymphs Heliconian springs ;
To caress the Royal Day,
That such a blessing did convey,
No less a blessing than the best of Kings...

When Kings, that make the publick good their care,
Advance in dignity and state,
Their rise no envy can create ;
Because their subjects in their grandeur share,
For like the sun, the higher they ascend,
The farther their indulgent beams extend.
Yet long before our Royal Sun
His destined course has run
We're blest to see a glorious Heir,
That shall the mighty loss repair,
When he that blazes now, shall this low sphere resign,
In a sublimer orb eternally to shine...

NICHOLAS ROWE Esq.

For I. Hinton at the Kings Arms in Newgate Street.

# NICHOLAS ROWE

## 1674–1718

With Rowe's appointment the laureateship regained some of the
status it had enjoyed under Dryden. Admittedly Rowe was a rather
dull, unexciting poet, but his plays were admired and he was pop-
ular as a man. He was at the height of his career when Nahum
Tate died in 1715. There was no hesitation over his appointment,
which was announced a week later.

By now the tradition of yearly odes had been established. To
mark the start of each New Year and on the sovereign's birthday
the laureate would deliver an ode which was set to music and
solemnly sung by the royal choir. It seems that George I was
indifferent to poetry, but there was a strong interest in music at
court. It is perhaps not surprising that Rowe's official odes are of
no great consequence ; his real interests and talents lay elsewhere.
His tragedy *Tamerlane*, a political allegory praising William of
England and attacking Louis XIV of France, had established him
as a dramatist. For many years it was performed annually at Drury
Lane on 5 November, the anniversary of King William's landing.

Rowe was a good linguist and a man of wide learning and schol-
arship. His pioneering edition of Shakespeare was a first attempt at
a critical edition of the plays. He also wrote the first life of Shake-
speare. His translation of Lucan's *Pharsalia* was described by Dr.
Johnson as "one of the greatest productions of English poetry".

Rowe was a witty and vivacious man, handsome and charming.
He was a close friend of Alexander Pope, who called him "the best
of men" and wrote his epitaph. Rowe died at home in Covent Gar-
den and was buried in Westminster Abbey.

# Song
### on a fine woman who had a dull husband

When on fair Celia's eyes I gaze,
　　And bless their light divine ;
I stand confounded with amaze,
　　To think on what they shine.

On one vile clod of earth she seems
　　To fix their influence ;
Which kindles not at those bright beams
　　Nor wakens into sense.

Lost and bewilder'd with the thought,
　　I could not but complain,
That Nature's lavish hand had wrought
　　This fairest work in vain.

Thus some who have the stars survey'd,
　　Are ignorantly led,
To think those glorious lamps were made
　　To light Tom Fool to bed.

## *from* Ode for the New Year, 1716

*This ode was addressed to King George I. The collapse of the first Jacobite Rebellion the year before may account for the poet laureate's hailing his very Hanoverian king as "thou great Plantagenet".*

Hail to thee, glorious rising Year,
With what uncommon grace thy days appear !
　　Comely art thou in thy prime,
　　Lovely child of hoary Time ;

Where thy golden footsteps tread,
Pleasures all around thee spread ;
Bliss and beauty grace thy train ;
Muse, strike the lyre to some immortal strain.
But, Oh ! what skill, what master hand,
Shall govern or constrain the wanton band ?
Loose like my verse they dance, and all without command.
Images of fairest things
Crowd about the speaking strings ;
Peace and sweet prosperity,
Faith and cheerful loyalty,
With smiling love and deathless poesy.


Ye scowling shades who break away,
Well do ye fly and shun the purple day,
Every fiend and fiend-like form,
Black and sullen as a storm,
Jealous Fear, and false Surmise,
Danger with her dreadful eyes,


Faction, Fury, all are fled,
And bold Rebellion hides her daring head.
Behold, thou gracious Year, behold,
To whom thy treasures all thou shalt unfold,
For whom thy whiter days were kept from times of old !
See thy George, for this is he !
On his right hand waiting free,
Britain and fair Liberty.
Every good is in his face,
Every open honest grace.
Thou great Plantagenet ! immortal be thy race !

# Laurence Eusden

### 1688–1730

In rush'd Eusden and cry'd, who shall have it
But I, the true laureate, to whom the King gave it ?
Apollo begged pardon and granted his claim,
But vow'd that till then he'd never heard of his name.

Eusden was not at all like his predecessor Nicholas Rowe, who was a man of ability and reputation. He was little known, of no influence or standing. He never published a book of poems ; his work remains buried in old newspapers.

A fellow of Trinity College, Cambridge, Eusden wrote poems which were often tributes to the royal family, bidding for their notice and patronage. Robert Southey later remarked on his "strain of fulsome flattery in mediocre poetry". Eusden managed to attach himself to the Duke of Newcastle, who was to become Lord Chamberlain and so had the office of poet laureate in his gift.

This appointment provoked great mirth and ridicule. Pope (unfairly, it must be said) branded Eusden "a parson much bemused by beer". He had by now been ordained, and he took up the position of rector of Coningsby in Lincolnshire from where he sent his odes for performance at court. His last ode was performed after his death, news of which took a month to reach London, a month during which no one noticed that the poet laureate was missing.

## Ode for the New Year
### sung before the King, January 1, 1719–20

*Eusden's ode was addressed to George I. The sentiments of his poet laureate were impeccable, his verses less so.*

### Recit.

Lift up thy hoary Head and rise,
  Thou mighty Genius of this Isle !
Around thee cast thy wond'ring Eyes,
  See all thy Albion smile.
Mirth's Goddess her blest Pow'r maintains ;
  In Cities, Courts, and Rural Plains
Brunswick, the Glorious Brunswick reigns !

### Air

Now forbear, forbear to languish,
Cheerful rouse from needless Anguish ;
For Pleasures now are ever growing,
Tho' thy kind Eyes were once o'erflowing
Our too impending Dangers knowing.
The Days, the Nights were spent in groaning,
Poor Britannia's Fate bemoaning.

*Recit.*

Let the young dawning Year a George resound,
A George's Fame can fill its spacious Round!
Here every Virtue pleas'd thou may'st behold
Which rais'd a Hero to a God of old;
To form this One, the mix'd Ideas draw
From Edward, Henry, and the Lov'd Nassau...

*Chorus*

Genius!  Now securely rest,
For we now are ever blest;
Thou thy Guardianship may'st spare,
Britain is a Brunswick's Care.

# COLLEY CIBBER

1671–1757

It was not immediately obvious who would succeed Eusden when he died in 1730. Richard Savage, on the promise of an annual birthday ode for Queen Caroline, had already taken the title "volunteer laureate". Other contenders were Stephen Duck, "Honest Duck", a Wiltshire farm labourer, the critic Lewis Theobald, and the dramatist Colley Cibber.

The son of a sculptor originally from Holstein, Cibber had joined his father in the army that welcomed William of Orange but, when he failed to get a commission, he made his way to London. He became a member of the company at the Theatre Royal, but actors were often not paid for months on end and he decided to write his own play. *Love's Last Shift*, in which he played Sir Novelty Fashion, was well received, and for the next thirty years Cibber had great success as a playwright, actor and manager. He had a weak voice, and in his young days he was known by the name "Hatchet Face", so it is perhaps not surprising that he did best in comic roles. His play *The Non-Juror*, which satirized the Jacobites, was his passport to the laureateship.

His appointment was greeted with derision, particularly by Pope, who made Cibber the hero of his *Dunciad*. It is true that his twenty-six official odes set a new standard for banality and empty flattery: George II was not an easy king to praise. Cibber knew they were poor and met any criticism of them with unshakeable good humour. When his first ode was attacked, he joined in with a set of anonymous verses criticizing it. The post he had inherited from Eusden was by now regarded as something

of a joke and he did nothing to improve it. He placed little impor-
tance on a job that entailed producing verses twice a year to be
sung by the boys of the Chapel Royal. "I wrote more to be fed
than to be famous," he said.

## Song

*Cibber wrote this song in 1697 for his play* Woman's Wit, or the Lady
in Fashion.

> Tell me, *Belinda*, prithee do,
>    (The wanton Caelia said)
> Since you'll allow no lover true,
>    (Inform a tender Maid)
> Are not we Women Fools then to be so ?
> *Belinda* smiling thus her sex betray'd :

>    Men have their Arts, and we have Eyes,
>    We both believe, and both tell Lies ;
>    Tho' they a thousand Hearts pursue,
>    We love to wound as many too.

> Yet still with Virtue ! Virtue ! Virtue ! keep a Pother,
>    We look ! We love !
>    We like ! We leave !
>    We doth deceive !
> And thus are Fools to one another.

## What tho' they call me Country Lass

*A gay little song from Cibber's play* The Provok'd Husband.

What tho' they call me Country Lass,
   I read it plainly in my Glass,
   That for a Duchess I might pass :
   Oh, could I see the Day !
Would Fortune but attend my Call,
At Park, at Play, at Ring and Ball,
I'd brave the proudest of them all,
    With a *Stand-by—Clear the Way.*

Surrounded by a Crowd of Beaux,
With smart Toupees, and powder'd Clothes,
At Rivals I'd turn up my Nose ;
   Oh, could I see the Day !
I'll dart such Glances from these Eyes,
Shall make some Lord or Duke my Prize ;
And then Oh ! how I'll tyrannize,
    With a *Stand-by—Clear the Way.*

Oh ! then for every new Delight
For Equipage and Diamonds bright,
*Quadrille*, and Plays, and Balls all Night ;
   Oh, could I see the Day !
Of Love and Joy I'd take my Fill
The tedious Hours of Life to Kill,
In ev'ry thing I'd have my Will,
    With a *Stand-by—Clear the Way.*

# Birthday Ode
## (October 28, 1732)

*The birthday ode that Cibber produced for George II in 1732 set a new
standard for banality and empty flattery.*

Let there be light !
Such was at once the word and work of heav'n,
  When from the void of universal night
  Free nature sprung to the Creator's sight,
And day to glad the new-born world was giv'n.

Succeeding days to ages, roll'd,
And ev'ry age some wonder told :
At length arose this glorious morn !
  When, to extend his bounteous pow'r,
  High heav'n announce'd this instant hour
The best of monarchs shall be born !

  Born to protect and bless the land !
And while the laws his people form,
His scepter glorious to confirm
  Their wishes are his sole command.

The word that form'd the world
  In vain did make mankind ;
Unless, his passions to restrain,
  Almighty wisdom had design'd
Sometimes a WILLIAM, or a GEORGE should reign.

Yet farther, *Britons*, cast your eyes,
Behold a long succession rise
Of future fair felicities.

Around the royal table spread,
See how the beauteous branches shine !
Sprung from the fertile genial bed
Of glorious GEORGE and CAROLINE.

# WILLIAM WHITEHEAD

When Cibber's twenty-seven-year reign ended, it was hoped that the good name of the laureateship could be restored by the appointment of a poet with some quality. Hopes were pinned on Thomas Gray but, when he refused, George II and his court gave the matter little more thought and appointed William Whitehead.

Whitehead's father was a Cambridge baker who spent a lot of time and money ornamenting his garden, "Whitehead's Folly", in Grantchester. William was a respectable and rather dull dramatist and writer of quite agreeable miscellaneous verse. His laureate odes would be no better or no worse than any one else's. He admired and imitated Pope, but his heroic couplets did not protect him from criticism. Just as Pope had pilloried Cibber, so Charles Churchill mocked Whitehead, but sadly Churchill had not Pope's ability to bestow immortality on his victims. Whitehead took criticism well. He was a good-humoured, amiable man. Although he was dependent all his life on the indulgence and support of others, he managed to avoid servility and flattery.

He was a conscientious laureate. His odes were poor, but they were an improvement on Cibber's. Whitehead saw himself as spokesman for the whole country, not for only one faction or party. He reflected the nation's mood at this time, a mood coloured by the rebellion of the American colonies and the war in Europe. He saw no need to defend the King or support the government. One hundred years had passed since Dryden had been appointed to the post of poet laureate, which he had filled with such distinction. By now it was taken for granted that the laureate's official poems would have little power to sway opinion or effect change.

## Song for Ranelagh

*Whitehead here is addressing the "belles" and "flirts" to be found at the
public gardens in Chelsea where fashionable society met and promenaded.*

Ye belles, and ye flirts, and ye pert little things,
    Who trip in this frollicsome round,
Pray tell me from whence this impertinence springs,
    The sexes at once to confound ?
What means the cock'd hat, and the masculine air,
    With each motion design'd to perplex ?
Bright eyes were intended to languish, not stare,
    And softness the test of your sex.

The girl, who on beauty depends for support,
    May call every art to her aid ;
The bosom display's and the petticoat short,
    Are samples she gives of her trade.
But you, on whom fortune indulgently smiles,
    And whom pride has preserved from the snare,
Should slyly attack us with coyness and wiles,
    Not with open, and insolent war.

The Venus, whose statue delights all mankind,
    Shrinks modestly back from the view,
And kindly should seem by the artist design'd
    To serve as a model for you.
Then learn, with her beauty, to copy her air,
    Nor venture too much to reveal :
Our fancies will paint what you cover with care,
    And double each charm you conceal.

The blushes of morn, and the mildness of May,
    Are charms which no art can procure :
O be but yourselves and our homage we pay,
    And your empire is solid and sure.
But if, Amazon like, you attack your gallants,
    And put us in fear of our lives,
You may do very well for sisters and aunts,
    But, believe me, you'll never be wives.

## Birthday Ode

*Whitehead's first birthday ode to the new king, George III.*

O, called by Heaven to fill that awful throne,
Where *Edward, Henry, William, George* have shone,
(Where Love with Rev'rence, Laws with Power agree,
And 'tis each Subject's birthright to be free)
    The fairest wreaths already won
      Are but a prelude to the whole :
    Thy arduous race is *now* begun,
      And, starting from a nobler Goal,
    Heroes and Kings of Ages past
      Are Thy compeers :  extended high
    The Trump of Fame expects the blast,
      The radiant Lists before Thee lie,
The Field is time, the prize ETERNITY !
    Beyond Example's bounded light
    'Tis Thine to urge thy daring flight,
      And heights untry'd explore :
    O think what Thou alone can'st give,
    What blessings *Britain* may receive
      When YOUTH unites with POWER !

# Thomas Warton

1728–1790

Warton was the only laureate in the eighteenth century who was
not principally a dramatist : he was a poet in his own right. Nor
had he any particular political loyalties or allegiance deserving
reward. He was a don at Oxford for the greater part of his life,
although he did not take tutoring very seriously. His passion was
Gothic architecture and he spent his vacations travelling the coun-
try examining churches and castles.

Warton was Professor of Poetry at Oxford for ten years. His
lectures were on classical subjects, delivered in Latin. He wrote
and published a lot of verse, but little of any significance, although
it is worth noting that he wrote sonnets, a form rarely used at
this time except by Thomas Gray. He provided a regular supply
of laureate odes, but none had the delicacy of style of which he
was capable.

He wrote a number of books about Oxford including a guide-
book to the town and an anthology called *The Oxford Sausage*. He
deserves to be remembered as a critic. His *Observations on the
Faery Queen of Spenser* established his reputation in this field and
led to a friendship with Dr. Johnson. His *History of English Poetry*
was the first such work of its kind ; his edition of Milton's poetry
was an important literary landmark.

By middle age Warton had developed into a squat, red-faced
man, a beer drinker and pipe smoker in not always very clean
clothes, who, when he talked, "gabbled like a turkey". He once
confronted the King at chapel and would have been ejected had he

not managed to make himself known. He died of a stroke as he sat in the common room of his Oxford college. Wordsworth, Coleridge, Hazlitt and Lamb read and admired his work, but the judgement of another of his contemporaries has had more influence on his long-term reputation : "the gods had made him poetical, but not a poet".

## To the River Lodon

*In this sonnet Warton looks forward to Wordsworth and the Romantics and away from the traditional odes and elegies of his contemporaries.*

Ah ! what a weary race my feet have run,
Since first I trod thy banks with alders crown'd,
And thought my way was all through fairy ground,
Beneath thy azure sky, and golden sun :
Where first my Muse to lisp her notes begun !
While pensive Memory traces back the round,
Which fills the varied interval between ;
Much pleasure, more of sorrow, marks the scene.
Sweet native stream ! those skies and suns so pure
No more return, to cheer my evening road !
Yet still one joy remains, that not obscure,
Nor useless, all my vacant days have flow'd,
From youth's gay dawn to manhood's prime mature ;
Nor with the Muse's laurel unbestow'd.

## As when the demon of the Summer storm

*Warton wrote this birthday ode to King George III in 1788, after the King had recovered from a bout of insanity.*

As when the demon of the Summer storm
Walks forth the noontide landscape to deform,
Dark grows the vale, and dark the distant grove,
    And thick the bolts of angry Jove
    Athwart the wat'ry welkin glide,
And streams th' aerial torrent far and wide :
    If by short fits the struggling ray
    Should dart a momentary day,
    Th' illumin'd mountain glows awhile,
    By faint degrees the radiant glance
    Purples th' horizon's pale expanse,
    And gilds the gloom with hasty smile :
    Ah ! fickle smile, too swiftly past !
    Again resounds the sweeping blast,
    With hoarser din the demon howls ;
    Again the blackening concave scowls ;
Sudden the shades of the meridian night
Yield to the triumph of rekindling light ;
The reddening sun regains his golden sway ;
And Nature stands reveal'd in all her bright array.

Such was the changeful conflict that possess'd
With trembling tumult every British breast,
When Albion, towering in the van sublime
    Of Glory's march, from clime to clime
    Envied, belov'd, rever'd, renown'd,
Her brows with every blissful chaplet bound,
    When in her mid career of state,
    She felt her monarch's awful fate !
    Till Mercy from th' Almighty throne

Look'd down on man, and waving wide
    Her wreath, that, in the rainbow dyed,
    With hues of soften'd lustre shone,
    And bending from her sapphire cloud
    O'er regal grief benignant bow'd ;
    To transport turn'd a people's fears,
    And stay'd a people's tide of tears :
   Bade this blest dawn with beams auspicious spring,
   With hope serene, with healing on its wing ;
   And gave a Sovereign o'er a grateful land
Again with vigorous grasp to stretch the scepter'd hand.

# HENRY PYE

1745–1813

In 1790 Thomas Cowper was the obvious choice to succeed Warton, but George III, "Farmer George", found his ideal poet laureate in Henry Pye, a country gentleman who wrote about country sports and the joys of the countryside, even in the presence of world-shaking events—the growing unrest and demand for reform in England, the execution in 1793 of the French King Louis XVI. Pye was briefly a Member of Parliament, which ruined him financially. His appointment was probably a reward for his loyal support of Prime Minister Pitt in the House.

Pye wrote plays and translated from Latin and Greek, but his main object in life was to be recognized as a poet. He performed his duties as laureate very assiduously, having first arranged for the traditional gift of a butt of sack to be replaced by an annual cash payment of £27. He was a safe pair of hands, a poet who could be relied upon. He was, declared Byron, "eminently respectable in everything but his poetry". His odes were written as if to a formula ; they were irreproachably patriotic and ludicrously tame. When a subject of epic proportions presented itself, as with England's great victory at Trafalgar, he was unable to rise to it. The story is told of his reading to a regiment at an army camp ; before he was half way through, all the front ranks and many of the others within earshot had dropped their arms and fallen asleep.

His responsibilities eased in 1811 when George III again lost his mind and the traditional odes were no longer required. Before he retired to his villa at Pinner, Pye announced that he was planning to publish his selected works in six volumes. Happily death intervened.

## Nurtur'd in storms the infant year

*Pye managed to ignore the awful events going on around him.  In his ode
for the year 1793, which saw the execution of the French King Louis XVI
and growing demands for reform in England, he moves on very quickly to
more pleasing country matters.*

Nurtur'd in storms the infant year,
    Comes in terrific glory forth ;
Earth meets him wrapp'd in mantle drear,
    And the loud tempest sings his birth.
Yet 'mid the elemental strife
Brood the rich germs of vernal life,
Frore January's iron reign,
And the dark months succeeding train,
The renovated glebe prepare
For genial May's ambrosial air,
For fruits that glowing Summer yields,
For laughing Autumn's golden fields ;
    And the stout swain whose frame defies
    The driving storm, the hostile skies,
While his keen plowshare turns the stubborn soil,
Knows plenty only springs the just reward of toil.

## *from* On the Marriage of the Prince of Wales
## to Princess Caroline of Brunswick

*With a royal wedding Pye is in his element. He wrote this ode in 1795.*

O royal youth ! a king's, a parent's pride,
　　A nation's future hope !—again the tongue
That joined the choir, what time by Isis side
　　Her tuneful sons thy birth auspicious sung,
　Now hails, fulfill'd by Hymen's hallowed flame :
The warmest wish Affection's voice could frame :
　　　For say, can Fame, can Fortune know
　　　Such genuine raptures to bestow,
As from the smiles of wedded love arise,
When heavenly virtue beams from blushing Beauty's
　　　　　eyes ?

# ROBERT SOUTHEY

1774–1843

Southey is probably now best remembered as one of the "Lake Poets", friend of William Wordsworth and brother-in-law of Samuel Taylor Coleridge, whose family he generously sheltered and supported when Coleridge abandoned them. Son of a Bristol linen-draper, he was a passionate liberal in his youth, expelled from school for founding a magazine called *The Flagellant*, supporter of the French Revolution and of Coleridge's short-lived scheme to set up a pantisocracy, an egalitarian commune on the banks of the Susquehanna in New England. It was expected that he would be ordained but he chose to study law. This he would give up, determined to devote himself fully to writing. With his wife he moved to Keswick in the Lake District to be near Coleridge, and here he remained for the rest of his life.

Southey worked very hard and produced a great many poems and translations as well as lives of Chatterton and Nelson, a three-volume history of Brazil, and journalism. His long association with the *Quarterly Review* brought him his only regular income and cemented his relationship with Sir Walter Scott. On Pye's death in 1813, the poet laureateship was offered to Scott, who refused it but who, in turn, proposed Southey.

Glad of the salary, however small, Southey grew to dislike the post. He had no interest in the court and chose to remain at Keswick, refusing offers of jobs and of a baronetcy. He managed to avoid writing the New Year and birthday odes, but he was very active in producing odes for big public events. He claimed to have written more than any other laureate before him. None was very inspired or inspiring.  One of these official poems brought him unwelcome fame.  In the preface to "A Vision of Judgement", commemorating the death of George III, he attacked Byron, who responded with his parody "The Vision of Judgement", and went on to mock his attacker in "Don Juan".  But Byron could not help admiring Southey's good looks : "To have that poet's head and shoulders, I would almost have written his Sapphics."

## After Blenheim

*One of Southey's famous ballads, this looks back to the battle of Blenheim in 1704 and the Duke of Marlborough's great victory against the French.*

It was a summer evening,
    Old Kaspar's work was done,
And he before his cottage door
    Was sitting in the sun ;
And by him sported on the green
His little grandchild Wilhelmine.

She saw her brother Peterkin
    Roll something large and round
Which he beside the rivulet
    In playing there had found ;
He came to ask what he had found
That was so large and smooth and round.

Old Kaspar took it from the boy
    Who stood expectant by ;

And then the old man shook his head,
 And with a natural sigh
" 'Tis some poor fellow's skull," said he,
"Who fell in the great victory.

"I find them in the garden,
 For there 's many here about,
And often when I go to plough
 The ploughshare turns them out,
For many thousand men," said he
"Were slain in that great victory."

"Now tell us what 'twas all about,"
 Young Peterkin he cries ;
And little Wilhelmine looks up
 With wonder-waiting eyes ;
"Now tell us all about the war,
And what they fought each other for."

"It was the English," Kaspar cried,
 "Who put the French to rout ;
But what they fought each other for
 I could not well make out.
But everybody said," quoth he,
"That 'twas a famous victory.

"My father lived at Blenheim then,
 Yon little stream hard by ;
They burnt his dwelling to the ground,
 And he was forced to fly :

So with his wife and child he fled,
Nor had he where to rest his head.

"With fire and sword the country round
    Was wasted far and wide,
And many a childing mother then
    And new-born baby died :
But things like that, you know, must be
At every famous victory.

"They say it was a shocking sight
    After the field was won ;
For many thousand bodies here
    Lay rotting in the sun :
But things like that, you know, must be
After a famous victory.

"Great praise the Duke of Marlbro' won
    And our good Prince Eugene ;"
"Why, 'twas a very wicked thing !"
    Said little Wilhelmine ;
"Nay... nay... my little girl," quoth he,
"It was a famous victory.

"And everybody praised the Duke
    Who this great fight did win."
"But what good came of it at last ?"
    Quoth little Peterkin :
"Why, that I cannot tell," said he,
"But 'twas a famous victory."

## The Immortality of Love

*This is part of Southey's long poem* The Curse of Kehana, *published in 1810.*

They sin who tell us Love can die.
With life all other passions fly,
All others are but vanity.
In Heaven Ambition cannot dwell,
Nor Avarice in the vaults of Hell ;
Earthly these passions of the Earth,
They perish where they have their birth ;
But Love is undestructible.
Its holy flame for ever burneth,
From Heaven it came, to Heaven returneth ;
Too oft on Earth a troubled guest,
At times deceived, at times oppressed,
It here is tried and purified,
Then hath in heaven its perfect rest ;
It soweth here with toil and care,
But the harvest time of Love is there.
Oh ! when a mother meets on high
The Babe she lost in infancy,
Hath she not then, for pains and fears,
The day of woe, the watchful night,
For all her sorrow, all her tears,
An over-payment of delight ?

# The Well of St. Keyne

*Southey wrote a number of excellent ballads. This has a pleasing twist in the tail.*

A well there is in the west country,
  And a clearer one never was seen ;
There is not a wife in the west country
  But has heard of the Well of St. Keyne.

An oak and an elm-tree stand beside,
  And behind doth an ash-tree grow,
And a willow from the bank above
  Droops to the water below.

A traveller came to the Well of St. Keyne ;
  Joyfully he drew nigh,
For from cock-crow he had been travelling,
  And there was not a cloud in the sky.

He drank of the water so cool and clear,
  For thirsty and hot was he,
And he sat down upon the bank
  Under the willow-tree.

There came a man from the house hard by
  At the Well to fill his pail ;
On the Well-side he rested it,
  And he bade the stranger hail.

"Now art thou a bachelor, stranger ?"  quoth he,
  "For an if thou hast a wife,
The happiest draught thou hast drunk this day
  That ever thou didst in thy life.

"Or has thy good woman, if one thou hast,
 Ever here in Cornwall been ?
For an if she have, I'll venture my life
 She has drunk of the Well of St. Keyne."

"I have left a good woman who never was here,"
 The stranger he made reply,
"But that my draught should be the better for that,
 I pray you answer me why ?"

"St. Keyne," quoth the Cornish-man, "many a time
 Drank of this crystal Well,
And before the angel summoned her,
 She laid on the water a spell.

"If the husband of this gifted Well
 Shall drink before his wife,
A happy man thenceforth is he,
 For he shall be master for life.

"But if the wife should drink of it first,
 God help the husband then !"
The stranger stooped to the Well of St. Keyne,
 And drank of the water again.

"You drank of the Well I warrant betimes ?"
 He to the Cornish-man said :
But the Cornish-man smiled as the stranger spake,
 And sheepishly shook his head.

"I hastened as soon as the wedding was done,
 And left my wife in the porch ;
But i' faith she had been wiser than me,
 For she took a bottle to church."

## *from* An Ode for St. George's Day

*One of Southey's laureate poems, this ode is full of patriotic sentiment, with its many references to earlier successes against the French—at Crécy and Poitiers and Agincourt where Henry V led his men to a great victory on St. George's Day, 23 April 1415.*

…But thou, O England ! to that sainted name
Hast given its proudest praise, its loftiest fame.
Witness the field of Cressy, on that day,
When vollying thunders roll'd unheard on high,
For in that memorable fray
Broken, confused, and scatter'd in dismay,
France had ears only for the Conqueror's cry,
St. George, St. George for England ! St. George
and Victory !

Bear witness Poictiers ! where again the foe
From that same hand received his overthrow.
In vain essay'd, Mount Joye St. Denis rang
From many a boastful tongue,
And many a hopeful heart in onset brave ;
Their courage in the shock of battle quail'd
His dread response when sable Edward gave,
And England and St. George again prevail'd.

Bear witness Agincourt, where once again
The bannered lilies on the ensanguin'd plain
Were trampled by the fierce pursuers' feet ;
And France, doom'd ever to defeat

Against that foe, beheld her myriads fly
Before the withering cry,
St. George, St. George for England! St. George
        and Victory!


That cry in many a field of Fame
Through glorious ages held its high renown;
Nor less hath Britain proved the sacred name
        Auspicious to her crown.
Troubled too oft her course of fortune ran
        Till when the Georges came
            Her happiest age began.
Beneath their just and liberal sway,
Old feuds and factions died away;


One feeling through her realms were known,
One interest of the Nation and the Throne.
Ring, then, ye bells upon St. George's Day,
From every tower in glad accordance ring;
And let all instruments, full, strong, or sweet,
        With touch of modulated string,
And soft of swelling breath, and sonorous beat,
        The happy name repeat,
While heart and voice their joyous tribute bring
    And speak the People's love for George their King.

Alfred Croquis delt.

# WILLIAM WORDSWORTH

## 1770–1850

Wordsworth succeeded his old friend Robert Southey as poet laureate in 1843. At first he refused—he was nearly seventy-three, his life as a writer all but over—accepting only when he was promised that nothing would be required of him. He had been an important public figure for many years—Elizabeth Barrett Browning called him the "king-poet of our times"—but his poetic inspiration came from interaction with landscape and place, the exercise of memory, knowledge gained from his own experience.

Wordsworth's imaginative life was closely linked to the place of his birth and his early childhood, Cockermouth in the Lake District. Orphaned at the age of thirteen and separated from his brothers and sister, he went to school at Hawkshead, and then on to Cambridge. While a student he went on a walking tour of the Alps, travelling some 2000 miles through a country in revolution, where he discovered "human nature seeming born again". A year later, visiting the Loire, he fell in love with a young French woman with whom he had a daughter.

In 1797 he moved with his sister, Dorothy, to Alfoxden in Somerset to live near Coleridge. The two men wrote, walked, talked together, finding enormous stimulus and joy in each other's company. In one marvellous year, Coleridge wrote nearly all his greatest poems; together the two poets produced the *Lyrical Ballads*, aiming to show, Wordsworth wrote later, "that men who do not wear fine clothes can feel deeply", and he wrote one of his greatest poems, "Lines Written a Few Miles Above Tintern Abbey".

Shortly he would complete the first version of what would be *The Prelude*, which he referred to as "the poem for Coleridge".

Wordsworth, always with Dorothy, returned to the Lake District, first to Dove Cottage in Grasmere, settling finally at Rydal Mount. Marriage brought great happiness and children. Early hostile criticism of his poems changed to admiration and acceptance; the young democrat and Jacobin became a respected figure. He had by now outlived his young contemporaries, Byron, Shelley and Keats. Hazlitt and Browning lamented his loss of radical faith, but Matthew Arnold and John Stuart Mill revered him. He lived to see his work absorbed into the new age. Wordsworth believed the creative power to be a fundamental human attribute. He saw poetry as a moral agent: it was the duty of the poet to "rectify men's feelings". "He ought to travel before men occasionally as well as at their sides."

# Lines Written a Few Miles Above Tintern Abbey,
## on Revisiting the Banks of the Wye During a Tour, July 13, 1798

Five years have passed ; five summers, with the length
Of five long winters ! and again I hear
These waters rolling from their mountain-springs
With a sweet inland murmur.—Once again
Do I behold these steep and lofty cliffs,
Which on a wild secluded scene impress
Thoughts of more deep seclusion ; and connect
The landscape with the quiet of the sky.
The day is come when I again repose
Here, under this dark sycamore, and view
These plots of cottage-ground, these orchard-tufts,
Which, at this season, with their unripe fruits,
Among the woods and copses lose themselves,
Nor, with their green and simple hue, disturb
The wild green landscape.  Once again I see
These hedge-rows, hardly hedge-rows, little lines
Of sportive wood run wild ;  these pastoral farms
Green to the very door ;  and wreathes of smoke
Sent up, in silence, from among the trees,
With some uncertain notice, as might seem
Of vagrant dwellers in the houseless woods,
Or of some hermit's cave, where by his fire
The hermit sits alone.
                        Though absent long,
These forms of beauty have not been to me,
As is a landscape to a blind man's eye :

But oft, in lonely rooms, and mid the din
Of towns and cities, I have owed to them,
In hours of weariness, sensations sweet,
Felt in the blood, and felt along the heart,
And passing even into my purer mind
With tranquil restoration :—feelings too
Of unremembered pleasure ; such, perhaps,
As may have had no trivial influence
On that best portion of a good man's life ;
His little, nameless, unremembered acts
Of kindness and of love.  No less, I trust,
To them I may have owed another gift,
Of aspect more sublime ;  that blessed mood,
In which the burthen of the mystery,
In which the heavy and the weary weight
Of all this unintelligible world
Is lighten'd :—that serene and blessed mood,
In which the affections gently lead us on,
Until, the breath of this corporeal frame,
And even the motion of our human blood
Almost suspended, we are laid asleep
In body, and become a living soul :
While with an eye made quiet by the power
Of harmony, and the deep power of joy,
We see into the life of things.
                              If this
Be but a vain belief, yet, oh !  how oft,
In darkness, and amid the many shapes
Of joyless day-light :  when the fretful stir
Unprofitable, and the fever of the world,

Have hung upon the beatings of my heart,
How oft, in spirit, have I turned to thee
O sylvan Wye! Thou wanderer through the woods,
How often has my spirit turned to thee!

And now, with gleams of half-extinguish'd thought,
With many recognitions dim and faint,
And somewhat of a sad perplexity,
The picture of the mind revives again:
While here I stand, not only with the sense
Of present pleasure, but with pleasing thoughts
That in this moment there is life and food
For future years. And so I dare to hope
Though changed, no doubt, from what I was, when first
I came among these hills; when like a roe
I bounded o'er the mountains, by the sides
Of the deep rivers, and the lonely streams,
Wherever nature led; more like a man
Flying from something that he dreads, than one
Who sought the thing he loved. For nature then
(The coarser pleasures of my boyish days,
And their glad animal movements all gone by,)
To me was all in all.—I cannot paint
What then I was. The sounding cataract
Haunted me like a passion: the tall rock,
The mountain, and the deep and gloomy wood,
Their colours and their forms, were then to me
An appetite: a feeling and a love,
That had no need of a remoter charm,
By thought supplied, or any interest

Unborrowed from the eye.—That time is past,
And all its aching joys are now no more,
And all its dizzy raptures.  Not for this
Faint I, nor mourn nor murmur : other gifts
Have followed, for such loss, I would believe,
Abundant recompence.  For I have learned
To look on nature, not as in the hour
Of thoughtless youth, but hearing oftentimes
The still, sad music of humanity,
Not harsh nor grating, though of ample power
To chasten and subdue.  And I have felt
A presence that disturbs me with the joy
Of elevated thoughts ;  a sense sublime
Of something far more deeply interfused,
Whose dwelling is the light of setting suns,
And the round ocean, and the living air,
And the blue sky, and in the mind of man,
A motion and a spirit, that impels
All thinking things, all objects of all thought,
And rolls through all things.  Therefore am I still
A lover of the meadows and woods,
And mountains ;  and of all that we behold
From this green earth ;  of all the mighty world
Of eye and ear, both what they half-create,
And what perceive ;  well pleased to recognize
In nature and the language of the sense,
The anchor of my purest thoughts, the nurse,
The guide, the guardian of my heart, and soul
Of all my moral being.

                                    Nor, perchance,
If I were not thus taught, should I the more
Suffer my genial spirits to decay :
For thou art with me, here, upon the banks
Of this fair river ;  thou, my dearest Friend,
My dear, dear Friend, and in thy voice I catch
The language of my former heart, and read
My former pleasures in the shooting lights
Of thy wild eyes.  Oh !  yet a little while
May I behold in thee what I was once,
My dear, dear Sister !  And this prayer I make,
Knowing that Nature never did betray
The heart that loved her ;  'tis her privilege,
Through all the years of this our life, to lead
From joy to joy :  for she can so inform
The mind that is within us, so impress
With quietness and beauty, and so feed
With lofty thoughts, that neither evil tongues,
Rash judgments, nor the sneers of selfish men,
Nor greetings where no kindness is, nor all
The dreary intercourse of daily life,
Shall e'er prevail against us, or disturb
Our chearful faith that all which we behold
Is full of blessings.  Therefore let the moon
Shine on thee in thy solitary walk ;
And let the misty mountain winds be free
To blow against thee :  and in after years,
When these wild ecstasies shall be matured
Into a sober pleasure, when thy mind

Shall be a mansion for all lovely forms,
Thy memory be as a dwelling-place
For all sweet sounds and harmonies ; Oh ! then,
If solitude, or fear, or pain, or grief,
Should be thy portion, with what healing thoughts
O tender joy wilt thou remember me,
And these my exhortations ! Nor, perchance,
If I should be, where I no more can hear
Thy voice, nor catch from thy wild eyes these gleams
Of past existence, wilt thou then forget
That on the banks of this delightful stream
We stood together ; and that I, so long
A worshipper of Nature, hither came,
Unwearied in that service : rather say
With warmer love, oh ! with far deeper zeal
Of holier love. Nor wilt thou then forget,
That after many wanderings, many years
Of absence, these steep woods and lofty cliffs,
And this green pastoral landscape, were to me
More dear, both for themselves, and for thy sake.

## A slumber did my spirit seal

*One of Wordsworth's five "Lucy" poems, Lucy's identity has never been discovered.*

A slumber did my spirit seal
    I had no human fears :
She seem'd a thing that could not feel
    The touch of earthly years.

No motion has she now, no force ;
    She neither hears nor sees ;
Roll'd round in earth's diurnal course,
    With rocks, and stones and trees !

## Song

*Another of the "Lucy" poems, a simple moving elegy for an unknown girl.*

She dwelt among th' untrodden ways
    Beside the springs of Dove,
A Maid whom there were none to praise
    And very few to love.

A Violet by a mossy Stone
    Half-hidden from the Eye !
—Fair as a star when only one
    Is shining in the sky !

She *liv'd* unknown, and few could know
    When Lucy ceas'd to be ;
But she is in her Grave, and, oh !
    The difference to me.

## London, 1802

*Wordsworth wrote this sonnet on his return from France in 1802. In disgust with the viciousness and small-mindedness he found in England, he called on Milton, one of the poets he most admired, as an example of godliness, virtue and simplicity.*

Milton ! thou should'st be living at this hour :
England hath need of thee : she is a fen
Of stagnant waters : altar, sword and pen,
Fireside, the heroic wealth of hall and bower,
Have forfeited their ancient English dower
Of inward happiness. We are selfish men ;
Oh ! raise us up, return to us again :
And give us manners, virtue, freedom, power.
Thy soul was like a Star and dwelt apart :
Thou hadst a voice whose sound was like the sea ;
Pure as the naked heavens, majestic, free,
So didst thou travel on life's common way,
In chearful godliness ; and yet thy heart
The lowliest duties on itself did lay.

## I wandered lonely as a Cloud

*Wordsworth probably wrote this poem after seeing the daffodils that
grew on the edge of Ullswater. His wife, Mary, wrote the two last lines
of the poem.*

I wandered lonely as a Cloud
That floats on high o'er Vales and Hills,
When all at once I saw a crowd
A host of dancing Daffodils ;
Along the Lake, beneath the trees,
Ten thousand dancing in the breeze.

The waves beside them danced, but they
Outdid the sparkling waves in glee :—
A Poet could not but be gay,
In such a laughing company :
I gaz'd—and gaz'd—but little thought
What wealth the shew to me had brought :

For oft, when on my couch I lie
In vacant or in pensive mood,
They flash upon that inward eye
Which is the bliss of solitude,
And then my heart with pleasure fills,
And dances with the Daffodils.

## My heart leaps up when I behold

*Wordsworth used the last three lines of this poem as an epigraph for his ode
"Intimations of Immortality".*

> My heart leaps up when I behold
>    A rainbow in the sky :
> So was it when my life began ;
> So is it now I am a Man ;
> So be it when I shall grow old,
>    Or let me die !
> The Child is father of the Man ;
> And I could wish my days to be
> Bound each to each by natural piety.

## Ode

### Paulò majora canamus

*This ode is better known by the subtitle added later, "Intimations of Immor-
tality from Recollections of Early Childhood". In it Wordsworth celebrates
the power of memory, how it enables us to link our childhood and adult selves.*

> There was a time when meadow, grove, and stream,
> The earth, and every common sight,
>       To me did seem
>    Apparell'd in celestial light,
> The glory and the freshness of a dream.
> It is not now as it has been of yore ;—
>       Turn whereso'er I may,
>          By night or day,
> The things which I have seen I now can see no more.

     The Rainbow comes and goes,
     And lovely is the Rose,
     The Moon doth with delight
Look round her when the heavens are bare ;
     Waters on a starry night
     Are beautiful and fair ;
   The sunshine is a glorious birth ;
   But yet I know, where'er I go,
That there hath pass'd away a glory from the earth.

Now, while the Birds thus sing a joyous song,
    And while the young Lambs bound
     As to the tabor's sound,
To me alone there came a thought of grief :
A timely utterance gave that thought relief,
     And I again am strong :
The Cataracts blow their trumpets from the steep ;
No more shall grief of mine the season wrong ;
I hear the Echoes through the mountains throng,
The Winds come to me from the fields of sleep,
     And all the earth is gay,
       Land and sea
    Give themselves up to jollity,
     And with the heart of May
    Doth every Beast keep holiday,
      Thou Child of Joy,
Shout round me, let me hear thy shouts, thou happy
                  Shepherd Boy !

Ye blessed Creatures, I have heard the call
Ye to each other make ;  I see
The heavens laugh with you in your jubilee ;
My heart is at your festival,
My head hath its coronal,
The fulness of your bliss, I feel—I feel it all.
Oh evil day ! if I were sullen
While Earth herself is adorning,
This sweet May-morning,

And the Children are pulling
On every side,
In a thousand valleys far and wide,
Fresh flowers ;  while the sun shines warm,
And the Babe leaps up on his mother's arm :—
I hear, I hear, with joy I hear !
—But there's a Tree, of many one,
A single Field which I have look'd upon,
Both of them speak of something that is gone :
The Pansy at my feet
Doth the same tale repeat :
Wither is fled the visionary gleam ?
Where is it now, the glory and the dream ?

Broods like the Day, a Master o'er a Slave,
A Presence which is not to be put by ;
To whom the grave
Is but a lonely bed without the sense or sight
Of day or the warm light,

A place of thought where we in waiting lie ;
Thou little Child, yet glorious in the might
Of untam'd pleasures, on thy Being's height,
Why with such earnest pains dost thou provoke
The Years to bring the inevitable yoke,
Thus blindly with thy blessedness at strife ?
Full soon thy Soul shall have her earthly freight,
And custom lie upon thee with a weight,
Heavy as frost, and deep almost as life !

O joy ! that in our embers
Is something that doth live,
That nature yet remembers
What was so fugitive !
The thought of our past years in me doth breed
Perpetual benedictions :  not indeed
For that which is most worthy to be blest ;
Delight and liberty, the simple creed
Of Childhood, whether fluttering or at rest,
With new-born hope for ever in his breast :—
Not for these I raise
The song of thanks and praise ;
But for those obstinate questionings
Of sense and outward things,
Fallings from us, vanishings ;
Blank misgivings of a Creature
Moving about in worlds not realiz'd,
High instincts before which our mortal Nature
Did tremble like a guilty Thing surpriz'd :

But for those first affections,
Those shadowy recollections,
        Which, be they what they may,
Are yet the fountain light of all our day,
Are yet a master light of all our seeing;
        Uphold us, cherish us, and make
Our noisy years seem moments in the being
Of the eternal Silence: truths that wake,
        To perish never;
Which neither listlessness, nor mad endeavour,
        Nor Man nor Boy,
Nor all that is at enmity with joy,
Can utterly abolish or destroy!
        Hence in a season of calm weather,
        Though inland far we be,
Our Souls have sight of that immortal sea
        Which brought us hither,
        Can in a moment travel thither,
And see the Children sport upon the shore,
And hear the mighty waters rolling evermore.

Then, sing ye Birds, sing, sing a joyous song!
        And let the young Lambs bound
        As to the tabor's sound!
We in thought will join your throng,
        Ye that pipe and ye that play,
        Ye that through your hearts to-day
        Feel the gladness of the May!
What though the radiance which was once so bright

Be now for ever taken from my sight,
    Though nothing can bring back the hour
Of splendour in the grass, of glory in the flower ;
        We will grieve not, rather find
        Strength in what remains behind,
        In the primal sympathy
        Which having been must ever be,
        In the soothing thoughts that spring
        Out of human suffering,
        In the faith that looks through death,
In years that bring the philosophic mind.

And oh ye Fountains, Meadows, Hills, and Groves,
Think not of any severing of our loves !
Yet in my heart of hearts I feel your might :
I only have relinquished one delight
To live beneath your more habitual sway.
I love the Brooks which down their channels fret,
Even more than when I tripp'd lightly as they ;
The innocent brightness of a new-born Day
        Is lovely yet ;
The Clouds that gather round the setting sun
Do take a sober colouring from an eye
That hath kept watch o'er man's mortality ;
Another race hath been, and other palms are won.
Thanks to the human heart by which we live,
Thanks to its tenderness, its joys, and fears,
To me the meanest flower that blows can give
Thoughts that do often lie too deep for tears.

# Composed upon Westminster Bridge, Sept. 3, 1803

*Wordsworth's sonnet is a celebration of England. Although he lived for most of his life in the Lake District, he enjoyed visiting London and found much to admire there.*

Earth has not any thing to shew more fair :
Dull would he be of soul who could pass by
A sight so touching in its majesty :
This City now doth like a garment, wear
The beauty of the morning ;  silent, bare,
Ships, towers, domes, theatres, and temples lie
Open unto the fields, and to the sky ;
All bright and glittering in the smokeless air.
Never did sun more beautifully steep
In his first splendour, valley, rock, or hill ;
Ne'er saw I, never felt, a calm so deep !
The river glideth at his own sweet will ;
Dear God !  the very houses seem asleep ;
And all that mighty heart is lying still !

## The world is too much with us

*Wordsworth, the young democrat and supporter of the French Revolution, finds nothing as inspiring and liberating in the life of his own country.*

The world is too much with us ; late and soon,
Getting and spending, we lay waste our powers :
Little we see in nature that is ours ;
We have given our hearts away, a sordid boon !
This Sea that bares her bosom to the moon ;
The Winds that will be howling at all hours
And are up-gathered now like sleeping flowers ;
For this, for every thing, we are out of tune ;
It moves us not.  Great God !  I'd rather be
A Pagan suckled in a creed outworn ;
So might I, standing on this pleasant lea,
Have glimpses that would make me less forlorn ;
Have sight of Proteus coming from the sea ;
Or hear old Triton blow his wreathed horn.

# ALFRED, LORD TENNYSON

1809–1892

After Wordsworth's death, Prince Albert offered the laureateship to Samuel Rogers, by now aged eighty-seven, who wisely declined. There was talk of abolition, of the irrelevance of the post. It was suggested that Elizabeth Barrett Browning might be the ideal candidate. But Albert's next choice was Tennyson who, after a day and a night of deliberation, accepted. He was presented to the Queen some months later, uncomfortable in the court suit he had borrowed from Samuel Rogers, as Wordsworth had done before him.

Tennyson gave the poet laureateship new status and significance. There would be, apart from the Queen herself, no more fitting symbol of the Victorian age. He had many interests—science, the natural world, religion, politics and morality. He was the mirror through which the Victorians contemplated the best in themselves. He embodied and exquisitely expressed all the ideas of the day.

The year of his appointment—1850—was a pivotal one. It was the year when he finally married Emily Sellwood after a ten-year separation ; when he published *In Memoriam*, the elegy for his friend A. H. Hallam, which is one of his most important and most popular poems. In 1850 he put his restless, untidy youth behind him, the years haunted by his father's epilepsy and alcoholism, and was rewarded with a happy marriage and universal affection and respect.

He quickly discovered that the laureateship was no sinecure, that the laurel crown was more a crown of thorns. He was inundated with letters, poems, books, requests for help. He was approached, watched, observed wherever he went. But he also enjoyed a very busy social life and he liked to be hero-worshipped. He accepted a baronetcy, he said, only for the sake of his son Hallam, who had given up his own career to work with his parents.

Tennyson's death in 1892 marked an ending. It was felt that no one would ever again so well represent Victorian England. The great and the good attended his funeral service in Westminster Abbey—Thomas Hardy and Conan Doyle ; Burne-Jones and Millais ; Ellen Terry and Henry Irving. There were flowers from the Queen and from Gladstone ; a wreath from Shakespeare's garden, one from Delphi and one from Virgil's tomb. As a mark of respect, it was decided to leave the office of poet laureate vacant.

# The Lady of Shalott

*One of Tennyson's most popular poems, in which he questions the relationship in life of art and reality.*

On either side the river lie
Long fields of barley and of rye,
That clothe the world and meet the sky:
And thro' the field the road runs by
    To many-tower'd Camelot;
And up and down the people go,
Gazing where the lilies blow
Round an island there below,
    The island of Shalott.

Willows whiten, aspens quiver,
Little breezes dusk and shiver
Thro' the wave that runs for ever
By the island in the river
    Flowing down to Camelot.
Four gray walls, and four gray towers,
Overlook a space of flowers,
And the silent isle imbowers
    The Lady of Shalott.

By the margin, willow-veil'd,
Slide the heavy barges trail'd
By slow horses ;  and unhail'd
The shallop flitteth silken-sail'd
        Skimming down to Camelot :
But who hath seen her wave her hand ?
Or at the casement seen her stand ?
Or is she known in all the land
        The Lady of Shalott ?

Only reapers, reaping early
In among the bearded barley
Hear a song that echoes cheerly
From the river winding clearly
        Down to tower'd Camelot :
And by the moon the reaper weary,
Piling sheaves in uplands airy,
Listening, whispers " 'Tis the fairy
        Lady of Shalott."

There she weaves by night and day
A magic web with colours gay.
She has heard a whisper say,
A curse is on her if she stay
        To look down to Camelot.
She knows not what the curse may be,
And so she weaveth steadily
And little other care hath she,
        The Lady of Shalott.

And moving thro' a mirror clear
That hangs before her all the year,
Shadows of the world appear.
There she sees the highway near
  Winding down to Camelot:
There the river eddy whirls,
And there the surly village-churls,
And the red cloaks of market girls,
  Pass onward from Shalott.

Sometimes a troop of damsels glad,
An abbot on an ambling pad,
Sometimes a curly shepherd-lad,
Or long-hair'd page in crimson clad,
  Goes by to tower'd Camelot;
And sometimes thro' the mirror blue
The knights come riding two and two:
She hath no loyal knight and true,
  The Lady of Shalott.

But in her web she still delights
To weave the mirror's magic sights,
For often thro' the silent nights
A funeral, with plumes and lights
  And music, went to Camelot:
Or when the moon was overhead,
Came two young lovers lately wed;
"I am half sick of shadows," said
  The Lady of Shalott.

A bow-shot from her bower-eaves,
He rode between the barley-sheaves,
The sun came dazzling thro' the leaves,
And flamed upon the brazen greaves
        Of bold Sir Lancelot.
A red-cross knight for ever kneel'd
To a lady in his shield,
That sparkled on the yellow field,
        Beside remote Shalott.

The gemmy bridle glitter'd free,
Like some branch of stars we see
Hung in the golden Galaxy.
The bridle bells rang merrily
        As he rode down to Camelot:
And from his blazon'd baldric slung
A mighty silver bugle hung,
And as he rode his armour rung,
        Beside remote Shalott.

All in the blue unclouded weather
Thick-jewell'd shone the saddle-leather,
The helmet and the helmet-feather
Burn'd like one burning flame together.
        As he rode down to Camelot.
As often thro' the purple night
Below the starry clusters bright,
Some bearded meteor, trailing light
        Moves over still Shalott.

His broad clear brow in sunlight glow'd ;
On burnished hooves his war-horse trode ;
From underneath his helmet flow'd
His coal-black curls as on he rode,
     As he rode down to Camelot.
From the bank and from the river
He flash'd into the crystal mirror,
"Tirra lirra," by the river
     Sang Sir Lancelot.

She left the web, she left the loom,
She made three paces thro' the room,
She saw the water-lily bloom,
She saw the helmet and the plume,
     She look'd down to Camelot.
Out flew the web and floated wide ;
The mirror crack'd from side to side ;
"The curse is come upon me," cried
     The Lady of Shalott.

In the stormy east-wind straining,
The pale yellow woods were waning,
The broad stream in his banks complaining,
Heavily the low sky raining
     Over tower'd Camelot ;
Down she came and found a boat
Beneath a willow left afloat,
And round about the prow she wrote
     *The Lady of Shalott.*

And down the river's dim expanse
Like some bold seer in a trance,
Seeing all his own mischance—
With a glassy countenance
  Did she look to Camelot.
And at the closing of the day
She loosed the chain, and down she lay ;
The broad stream bore her far away,
  The Lady of Shalott.

Lying, robed in snowy white
That loosely flew to left and right—
The leaves upon her falling light—
Thro' the noises of the night
  She floated down to Camelot :
And as the boat-head wound along
The willowy hills and fields among,
They heard her sing her last song,
  The Lady of Shalott.

Heard a carol, mournful, holy
Chanted loudly, chanted lowly,
Till her blood was frozen slowly,
And her eyes were darken'd wholly,
  Turn'd to tower'd Camelot.
For ere she reach'd upon the tide
The first house by the water-side,
Singing in her song she died,
  The Lady of Shalott.

Under tower and balcony,
By garden-wall and gallery,
A gleaming shape she floated by,
Dead-pale between the houses high,
    Silent into Camelot.
Out upon the wharfs they came,
Knight and burgher, lord and dame,
And round the prow they read her name,
    *The Lady of Shalott.*

Who is this ?  and what is here ?
And in the lighted palace near
Died the sound of royal cheer ;
And they cross'd themselves for fear,
    All the knights at Camelot :
But Lancelot mused a little space ;
He said, "She had a lovely face ;
God in his mercy lend her grace,
    The Lady of Shalott."

## *from* The Lotos-Eaters

*Tennyson based this poem on the story in Homer's* Odyssey *of Odysseus and his men who, having tasted the lotus, lost all wish to return home.*

"Courage!" he said, and pointed towards the land,
"This mounting wave will roll us shoreward soon."
In the afternoon they came unto a land
In which it seemed always afternoon.
All round the coast the languid air did swoon,
Breathing like one that hath a weary dream.
Full-faced above the valley stood the moon ;
And like a downward smoke, the slender stream
Along the cliff to fall and pause and fall did seem.

A land of streams !  some, like a downward smoke,
Slow-dropping veils of thinnest lawn, did go ;
And some thro' wavering lights and shadows broke,
Rolling a slumbrous sheet of foam below.
They saw the gleaming river seaward flow
From the inner land :  far off, three mountain-tops
Three silent pinnacles of aged snow,
Stood sunset-flush'd :  and, dew'd with showery drops,
Up-clomb the shadowy pine above the woven copse.

The charmed sunset linger'd low adown
In the red West :  thro' mountain clefts the dale
Was seen far inland, and the yellow down
Border'd with palm, and many a winding vale

And meadow, set with slender galingale ;
A land where all things always seem'd the same !
And round about the keel with faces pale,
Dark faces pale against that rosy flame,
The mild-eyed melancholy Lotos-eaters came.

Branches they bore of that enchanted stem,
Laden with flower and fruit, whereof they gave
To each, but whoso did receive of them,
And taste, to him the gushing of the wave
Far far away did seem to mourn and rave
On alien shores ;  and if his fellow spake,
His voice was thin, as voices from the grave ;
And deep-asleep he seem'd, yet all awake,
And music in his ears his beating heart did make.

They sat them down upon the yellow sand,
Between the sun and moon upon the shore ;
And sweet it was to dream of Fatherland,
Of child, and wife, and slave ;  but evermore
Most weary seem'd the sea, weary the oar,
Weary the wandering fields of barren foam.
Then someone said, "We will return no more" ;
And all at once they sang, "Our island home
Is far beyond the wave ;  we will no longer roam."

# Break, break, break

*Tennyson wrote these lines in 1842, shortly after the death of his dear friend Arthur Hallam.*

Break, break, break
   On thy cold grey stones, O Sea !
And I would that my tongue could utter
   The thoughts that arise in me.

O well for the fisherman's boy,
   That he shouts with his sister at play !
O well for the sailor lad,
   That he sings in his boat on the bay !

And the stately ships go on
   To their haven under the hill ;
But O for the touch of a vanish'd hand,
   And the sound of a voice that is still !

Break, break, break
   At the foot of thy crags, O Sea !
But the tender grace of a day that is dead
   Will never come back to me.

## The splendour falls on castle walls

*A song that Tennyson added to his long poem* The Princess, *a debate on the education of women.*

The splendour falls on castle walls
    And snowy summits old in story :
The long light shakes across the lakes,
    And the wild cataract leaps in glory.
Blow, bugle, blow, set the wild echoes flying,
Blow, bugle ;  answer, echoes, dying, dying, dying.

    O hark, O hear !  how thin and clear,
        And thinner, clearer, farther going !
    O sweet and far from cliff and scar
        The horns of Elfland faintly blowing !
Blow, let us hear the purple glens relying :
Blow, bugle ;  answers, echoes, dying, dying, dying.

    O love, they die in yon rich sky,
        They faint on hill or field or river :
    Our echoes roll from soul to soul,
        And grow for ever and for ever.
Blow, bugle, blow, set the wild echoes flying,
And answer, echoes, answer, dying, dying, dying.

## *from* In Memoriam A. H. H.

### OBIT MDCCCXXXIII

*Tennyson's memorial to his Cambridge friend and fellow-poet Arthur Hallam which he wrote in a series of separate elegies over seventeen years.*

### I

I held it truth, with him who sings
　　To one clear harp in divers tones,
　　That men may rise on stepping-stones
Of their dead selves to higher things.

But who shall so forecast the years
　　And find in loss a gain to match ?
　　Or reach a hand thro' time to catch
The far-off interest of tears ?

Let Love clasp Grief lest both be drown'd,
　　Let darkness keep her raven gloss :
　　Ah, sweeter to be drunk with loss,
To dance with death, to beat the ground,

Than that the victor Hours should scorn
　　The long result of love, and boast,
　　"Behold the man that loved and lost,
But all he was is overworn."…

2

Old Yew, which graspest at the stones
        That name the under-lying dead,
        Thy fibres net the dreamless head,
Thy roots are wrapt about the bones.

The seasons bring the flower again,
        And bring the firstling to the flock ;
        And in the dusk of thee, the clock
Beats out the little lives of men.

O not for thee the glow, the bloom,
        Who changest not in any gale,
        Nor branding summer suns avail
To touch thy thousand years of gloom :

And gazing on thee, sullen tree,
        Sick for thy stubborn hardihood,
        I seem to fail from out my blood
And grow incorporate into thee...

5

I sometimes hold it half a sin
        To put in words the grief I feel ;
        For words, like Nature, half reveal
And half conceal the Soul within.

But, for the unquiet heart and brain,
    A use in measured language lies ;
    The sad mechanic exercise,
Like dull narcotics, numbing pain.

In words, like weeds, I'll wrap me o'er,
    Like coarsest clothes against the cold :
    But that large grief which these enfold
Is given in outline and no more...

### 7

Dark house, by which once more I stand
    Here in the long unlovely street,
    Doors, where my heart was used to beat
So quickly, waiting for a hand.

A hand that can be clasp'd no more—
    Behold me, for I cannot sleep,
    And like a guilty thing I creep
At earliest morning to the door.

He is not here : but far away
    The noise of life begins again,
    And ghastly thro' the drizzling rain
On the bald street breaks the blank day...

### 27

I envy not in any moods
    The captive void of noble rage,
    The linnet born within the cage,
That never knew the summer woods :

I envy not the beast that takes
   His license in the field of time,
   Unfetter'd by the sense of crime,
To whom a conscience never wakes ;

Nor, what may count itself as blest,
   The heart that never plighted troth
   But stagnates in the weeds of sloth ;
Nor any want-begotten rest.

I hold it true, whate'er befall ;
   I feel it, when I sorrow most ;
   'Tis better to have loved and lost
Than never to have loved at all...

### 101

Unwatch'd, the garden bough shall sway,
   The tender blossom flutter down,
   Unloved, that beech will gather brown,
This maple burn itself away ;

Unloved, the sun-flower, shining fair,
   Ray round with flames her disk of seed,
   And many a rose-carnation feed
With summer spice the humming air ;

Unloved, by many a sandy bar,
   The brook shall babble down the plain,
   At noon or when the lesser wain
Is twisting round the polar star ;

Uncared for, gird the windy grove,
 And flood the haunts of hern and crake ;
 Or into silver arrows break
The sailing moon in creek and cove ;

Till from the garden and the wild
 A fresh association blow,
 And year by year the landscape grow
Familiar to the stranger's child ;

As year by year the labourer tills
 His wonted glebe, or lops the glades ;
 And year by year our memory fades
From all the circle of the hills...

### 106

Ring out, wild bells, to the wild sky,
 The flying cloud, the frosty light :
 The year is dying in the night ;
Ring out, wild bells, and let him die.

Ring out the old, ring in the new,
 Ring, happy bells, across the snow :
 The year is going, let him go ;
Ring out the false, ring in the true.

Ring out the grief that saps the mind,
 For those that here we see no more ;
 Ring out the feud of rich and poor,
Ring in redress to all mankind.

Ring out a slowly dying cause,
    And ancient forms of party strife ;
    Ring in the nobler modes of life,
With sweeter manners, purer laws.

Ring out the want, the care, the sin,
    The faithless coldness of the times ;
    Ring out, ring out my mournful rhymes,
But ring the fuller minstrel in.

Ring out false pride in place and blood,
    The civic slander and the spite ;
    Ring in the love of truth and right,
Ring in the common love of good.

Ring out old shapes of foul disease ;
    Ring out the narrowing lust of gold ;
    Ring out the thousand wars of old,
Ring in the thousand years of peace.

Ring in the valiant man and free,
    The larger heart, the kindlier hand ;
    Ring out the darkness of the land,
Ring in the Christ that is to be...

### 129

Dear friend, far off, my lost desire,
    So far, so near in woe and weal ;
    O loved the most, when most I feel
There is a lower and a higher ;

Known and unknown ; human, divine ;
  Sweet human hand and lips and eye ;
  Dear heavenly friend that canst not die,
Mine, mine, for ever, ever mine ;

Strange friend, past, present, and to be ;
  Love deeplier, darkier understood ;
  Behold, I dream a dream of good,
And mingle all the world with thee.


## *from* Ode on the Death of the Duke of Wellington

*Wellington, the victor at Waterloo, died in November 1852. Tennyson's ode was published two days before the state funeral.*

### I

Bury the Great Duke
  With an empire's lamentation,
Let us bury the Great Duke
  To the noise of the mourning of a mighty nation,
Mourning when their leaders fall,
Warriors carry the warrior's pall,
And sorrow darkens hamlet and hall.

### 2

Where shall we lay the man whom we deplore ?
Here, in streaming London's central roar.
Let the sound of those he wrought for,
And the feet of those he fought for,
Echo round his bones for evermore.

### 3

Lead out the pageant : sad and slow,
As fits an universal woe,
Let the long long procession go,
And let the sorrowing crowd about it grow,
And let the mournful martial music blow ;
The last great Englishman is low...

### 9

Peace, his triumph will be sung
By some yet unmoulded tongue
Far on in summers that we shall not see :
Peace, it is a day of pain
For one about whose patriarchal knee
Late the little children clung :
O peace, it is a day of pain
For one, upon whose hand and heart and brain
Once the weight and fate of Europe hung.
Ours the pain, be his the gain !
More than is of man's degree
Must be with us, watching here
At this, our great solemnity.
Whom we see not we revere ;
We revere, and we refrain
From talk of battles loud and vain,
And brawling memories all too free
For such a wise humility
As befits a solemn fane :
We revere, and while we hear

The tides of Music's golden sea
Setting toward eternity,
Uplifted high in heart and hope are we,
Until we doubt not that for one so true
There must be other nobler work to do
Than when he fought at Waterloo,
And Victor he must ever be.
For tho' the Giant Ages heave the hill
And break the shore, and evermore
Make and break, and work their will ;
Tho' world on world in myriad myriads roll
Round us, each with different powers,
And other forms of life than ours
What know we greater than the soul ?
Oh God and Godlike men we build our trust.
Hush, the Dead March wails in the people's ears :
The dark crowd moves, and there are sobs and tears :
The black earth yawns :  the mortal disappears ;
Ashes to ashes, dust to dust ;  he is gone who seem'd
            so great.—
Gone ;  but nothing can bereave him
Of the force he made his own
Being here, and we believe him
Something far advanced in State,
And that he wears a truer crown
Than any wreath that man can weave him.
Speak no more of his renown,
Lay your earthly fancies down,
And in the vast cathedral leave him.
God accept him, Christ receive him.

## The Charge of the Light Brigade

*Tennyson wrote and published this poem in December 1854, after reading*
*in* The Times *of the charge at Balaclava in the Crimea.*

Half a league, half a league,
   Half a league onward,
All in the valley of Death
   Rode the six hundred.
"Forward, the Light Brigade!
Charge for the guns!" he said :
Into the valley of Death
   Rode the six hundred.

"Forward, the Light Brigade!"
Was there a man dismay'd ?
Not tho' the soldier knew
   Some one had blunder'd :
Their's not to make reply,
Their's not to reason why,
Their's but to do and die :
Into the valley of Death
   Rode the six hundred.

Cannon to right of them,
Cannon to left of them,
Cannon in front of them
   Volley'd and thunder'd ;
Storm'd at with shot and shell,

Boldly they rode and well,
Into the jaws of Death.
Into the mouth of Hell
    Rode the six hundred.

Flash'd all their sabres bare,
Flash'd all they turn'd in air
Sabring the gunners there,
Charging an army, while
    All the world wonder'd :
Plunged in the battery smoke
Right thro' the line they broke ;
Cossack and Russian
Reel'd from the sabre-stroke
    Shatter'd and sunder'd.
Then they rode back, but not
    Not the six hundred.

Cannon to right of them,
Cannon to left of them,
Cannon behind them.
    Volley'd and thunder'd ;
Storm'd at with shot and shell,
While horse and hero fell,
They that had fought so well
Came thro' the jaws of Death,
Back from the mouth of Hell,
All that was left of them,
    Left of six hundred.

When can their glory fade ?
O the wild charge they made !
　　All the world wonder'd.
Honour the charge they made !
Honour the Light Brigade,
　　Noble six hundred !


## *from* On the Jubilee of Queen Victoria

*One of Tennyson's laureate poems, which celebrates the Queen's Golden Jubilee in 1887.*

Fifty times the rose has flower'd and faded,
Fifty times the golden harvest fallen,
Since our Queen assumed the globe, the sceptre.

　　She beloved for a kindliness
　　Rare in Fable or History,
　　Queen, and Empress of India,
　　Crown'd so long with a diadem
　　Never worn by a worthier,
　　Now with prosperous auguries
　　Comes at last to the bounteous
　　Crowning year of her Jubilee.

Nothing of the lawless, of the Despot,
Nothing of the vulgar, or vainglorious,
All is gracious, gentle, great and Queenly.

You then joyfully, all of you,
Set the mountain aflame to-night,
Shoot your stars to the firmament,
Deck your houses, illuminate
All your towns for a festival,
And in each let a multitude
Loyal, each, to the heart of it,
One full voice of allegiance,
Hail the fair ceremonial
Of this year of her Jubilee...

You, the Mighty, the Fortunate,
You, the Lord-territorial,
You, the Lord-manufacturer,
You, the hardy, laborious,
Patient children of Albion,
You, Canadian, Indian,
Australasian, African,
All your hearts be in harmony,
All your voices be in unison,
Singing "Hail to the glorious
Golden year of her Jubilee !"

Are there thunders moaning in the distance ?
Are there spectres moving in the darkness ?
Trust the Hand of Light will lead her people,
Till the thunders pass, the spectres vanish,
And the Light is Victor, and the darkness
Dawns into the Jubilee of the Ages.

## Crossing the Bar

*Tennyson wrote this after he had recovered from a serious illness.   He wished it to appear at the end of all editions of his poems.*

Sunset and evening star,
    And one clear call for me !
And may there be no moaning of the bar,
    When I put out to sea,

But such a tide as moving seems asleep,
    Too full for sound and foam,
When that which drew from out the boundless deep
    Turns again home.

Twilight and evening bell,
    And after that the dark !
And may there be no sadness of farewell,
    When I embark ;

For tho' from out our bourne of Time and Place
    The flood may bear me far,
I hope to see my Pilot face to face
    When I have crost the bar.

# ALFRED AUSTIN

1835–1913

For four years after Tennyson's death there was much debate as to who might succeed him. Swinburne was rejected as too unreliable ; Kipling was thought unpredictable. Patmore might have stood a chance had he not already had three wives. Lord Salisbury wanted a poet sure to support the government, so Alfred Austin was chosen.

Poor Alfred Austin ! His is the first name in any list of the least successful poets laureate. He deserves better : we can admire him for two things at least. When he was living in Italy and discovered that Shelley's grave had been neglected, he tended it, planting pansies and violets and arranged for its upkeep. Later he established a fine garden at Swinford and in 1894 he published a very successful book on it called *The Garden That I Love*. And it must be said that some of his poems are charming, expressing a genuine and infectious enjoyment of nature and the outdoor world. In this he was a worthy successor to Tennyson.

Austin had been born in Headingley, the son of a prosperous wool merchant. He began writing at an early age—his first book, *Randolph*, subsidized by an uncle, sold seventeen copies. He trained as a lawyer and went on to the bar, but after a while he bought himself a cottage in the country and left for Rome. He spent some years abroad, writing all the while. Back home, he tried and failed to get into parliament, and became a newspaper leader writer instead. He kept on writing poetry and plays, and by the time of his appointment as poet laureate in early 1897, his collected works filled seven volumes.

Austin's reign started badly when he rushed into print with a poem celebrating the Jameson Raid, an incident in the Boer War soon seen as a fiasco and an embarrassment. In future he carefully avoided politics, but he loved hobnobbing in private with statesmen such as Metternich and Chamberlain. He was a rather pompous man with none of his predecessor's ability to speak to and for the whole country. During his years as laureate, poetry began to be the concern of the minority. Austin was not the man to stem this decline, as Tennyson would surely have done.

# Love's Unity

*Austin's sonnet is reminiscent of Elizabeth Barrett Browning's* Sonnets from the Portuguese, *and bears comparison with them.*

How can I tell thee when I love thee best ?
In rapture or repose ?  how shall I say ?
I only know I love thee every way,
Plumed for love's flight, or folded in love's nest,
See, what is day but night bedewed with rest ?
And what the night except the tired-out day ?
And 'tis love's difference, not love's decay,
If now I dawn, now fade, upon the breast.
Self-torturing sweet !  Is't not the self-same sun
Wanes in the west that flameth in the east,
His fervour nowise altered nor decreased ?
So rounds my love, returning where begun,
And still beginning, never most nor least,
But fixedly various, all love's parts in one.

# As Dies the Year

*Austin at his best, a lover and poet of the English countryside.*

The Old Year knocks at the farmhouse door.
    October, come with your matron gaze,
    From the fruit you are storing for winter days,
And prop him up on the granary floor,

Where the straw lies threshed and the corn
stands heaped :
Let him eat of the bread he reaped ;
He is feeble and faint, and can work no more.

Weaker he waneth, and weaker yet.
November, shower your harvest down,
Chestnut, and mast, and acorn brown ;
For you he laboured, so pay the debt.
Make him a pallet—he cannot speak—
And a pillow of moss for his pale pinched cheek,
With your golden leaves for coverlet.

He is numb to touch, he is deaf to call.
December, hither with muffled tread,
And gaze on the Year, for the Year is dead,
And over him cast a wan white pall.
Take down the mattock, and ply the spade.
And deep in the clay let his clay be laid,
And snowflakes fall at his funeral.

Thus may I die, since it must be,
My wage well earned and my work-days done,
And the seasons following one by one
To the slow sweet end that the wise foresee ;
Fed from the store of my ripened sheaves,
Laid to rest on my fallen leaves,
And with snow-white souls to weep for me.

## Sonnet Written in Mid-Channel

*Austin demonstrates the sturdy patriotism which perhaps contributed to his selection as laureate, and would surely have pleased his contemporaries.*

Now upon English soil I soon shall stand,
Homeward from climes that fancy deems more fair ;
And well I know that there will greet me there
No soft foam fawning upon smiling strand,
No scent of orange-groves, no zephyrs bland,
But Amazonian March, with breast half bare
And sleety arrows whistling through the air,
Will be my welcome from that burly land.
Yet he who boasts his birthplace yonder lies,
Owns in his heart a mood akin to scorn
For sensuous slopes that bask 'neath Southern skies,
Teeming with wine, and prodigal of corn,
And, gazing through the mist with misty eyes,
Blesses the brave bleak land where he was born.

## *from* Victoria

### May 24, 1819 – January 22, 1901

*Written after the Queen's death in January 1901. Austin would also outlive her successor, Edward VII, and would mourn him in equally extravagant terms.*

Dead! and the world feels widowed! Can it be
That she who scarce but yesterday upheld
The dome of empire, so the twain seemed one,
Whose goodness shone and radiated round
The circle of her still expanding rule,
Whose sceptre was self-sacrifice, whose throne
Only a loftier height from which to scan
The purpose of her people, their desires,
Thoughts, hopes, fears, needs, joys, sorrows, sadnesses,
Their strength in weal, their comforter in woe—
That this her mortal habitation should
Lie cold and tenantless! Alas! Alas!
Too often life has to be taught by death
The meaning and the pricelessness of love,
Not understood till lost. But she—but she
Was loved as monarch ne'ever was loved before
From girlhood unto womanhood, and grew,
Fresh as the leaf, and fragrant as the flower,
In grace and comeliness until the day
Of happy nuptial, glad maternity,
More closely wedded to her people's heart,
By each fresh tie that knitted her to him,

Whose one sole thought was how she still might be
Helpmate to England ;  England then, scarce more,
Or bounded by the name of British realm,
But by some native virtue broadening out
Into an empire wider than all names,
Till, like some thousand-years' out-branching oak,
Its mildness overshadowed half the globe
With peaceful arms and hospitable leaves.

# ROBERT BRIDGES

1844–1930

Bridges is most often remembered as the friend and first editor of the poems of Gerard Manley Hopkins. They met when students at Oxford and were lifelong correspondents. Bridges shared Hopkins's interest in new poetic rhythms and forms. His own poems, which have aged less well than those of his friend, are finely crafted and evidence of his wish to loosen the rhythms of verse and to write by new rules.

Bridges was a man astride two ages. Heir to the Victorians, he was born into wealth and privilege, a natural aristocrat, handsome, athletic, individualistic, aloof. He trained and worked as a doctor but he had no intention of working all his life. In 1881 he married and retired to the country. From then on his only employment was poetry and the study of music and language.

He was fortunate in being able to choose the course of his life, but he used his freedom well. Poet, philosopher, naturalist, musician, philologist, typographer, country gentleman—in everything he looked for and celebrated the true and the beautiful. But his deliberate seclusion, his isolation from what he saw as ugly and irrelevant, did not make for popular poetry, poetry rich in life or strong in feeling. W. B. Yeats said of one of his poems, "Every metaphor, every thought a commonplace, emptiness everywhere, the whole magnificent".

Bridges did not court the poet laureateship. He had no wish for popular applause or for fame. Dubbed "the dumb laureate", he was unmoved by criticism or attack. He wrote very few official poems. His first, "Noel : Christmas Eve, 1913", was published at the express wish of King George V. Bridges surprised both his admirers and his critics when, on his eighty-fifth birthday, he published "The Testament of Beauty", a very long philosophical poem in what he called "loose alexandrines". He remains a shadowy figure, partly because he destroyed his papers before his death to deter biographers. He was content to be a poet and felt no need to be anything else.

## Triolet

*Bridges had a particular interest in verse style and forms. This is a poem of eight lines with a distinctive rhyme pattern.*

When first we met we did not guess
That Love would prove so hard a master ;
Of more than common friendliness
When first we met we did not guess.
Who could foretell this sore distress,
This irretrievable disaster
When first we met !—We did not guess
That Love would prove so hard a master.

# A Passer-By

*One of Bridges's best-known lyric poems.*

Whither, O splendid ship, thy white sails crowding,
    Leaning across the bosom of the urgent West,
That fearest nor sea rising, nor sky clouding,
    Whither away, fair rover, and what thy quest ?

    Ah ! soon, when Winter has all our vales opprest,
When skies are cold and misty, and hail is hurling,
    Wilt thóu glide on the blue Pacific, or rest
In a summer haven asleep, thy white sails furling.

I there before thee, in the country that well thou knowest,
    Already arrived am inhaling the odorous air :
I watch thee enter unerringly where thou goest,
    And anchor queen of the strange shipping there,
    Thy sails for awnings spread, thy masts bare ;
Nor is aught from the foaming reef to the snow-capped, grandest
    Peak, that is over the feathery palms more fair
Than thou, so upright, so stately, and still thou standest.

And yet, O splended ship, unhailed and nameless,
    I know not if, aiming a fancy, I rightly divine
That thou hast a purpose joyful, a courage blameless,
    Thy port assured in a happier land than mine.
    But for all I have given thee, beauty enough is thine,
As thou, aslant with trim tackle and shrouding,
    From the proud nostril curve of a prow's line
In the offing scatterest foam, thy white sails crowding.

# London Snow

*One of Bridges's poems that shows the influence of his friend and fellow-poet Gerald Manley Hopkins.*

When men were all asleep the snow came flying,
In large white flakes falling on the city brown,
Stealthily and perpetually settling and loosely lying,
 Hushing the latest traffic of the drowsy town ;
Deadening, muffling, stifling its murmurs failing ;
Lazily and incessantly floating down and down :
 Silently sifting and veiling road, roof and railing ;
Hiding difference, making unevenness even,
Into angles and crevices softly drifting and sailing.
 All night it fell, and when full inches seven
It lay in the depth of its uncompacted lightness,
The clouds blew off from a high and frosty heaven ;
 And all woke earlier for the unaccustomed brightness
Of the winter dawning, the strange unheavenly glare :
The eye marvelled—marvelled at the dazzling whiteness ;
 The ear hearkened to the stillness of the solemn air ;
No sound of wheel rumbling nor of foot falling,
And the busy morning cries came thin and spare.
 Then boys I heard, as they went to school, calling,
They gathered up the crystal manna to freeze
Their tongues with tasting, their hands with snowballing ;
 Or rioted in a drift, plunging up to the knees ;
Or peering up from under the white-mossed wonder,

"O look at the trees !" they cried, "O look at the trees !"
   With lessened load a few carts creak and blunder,
Following along the white deserted way,
A country company long dispersed asunder :
   When now already the sun, in pale display
Standing by Paul's high dome, spread forth below
His sparkling beams, and awoke the stir of the day.
   For now doors open, and war is waged with the snow ;
And trains of sombre men, past tale of number,
Tread long brown paths, as toward their toil they go :
   But even for them awhile no cares encumber
Their minds diverted ; the daily word is unspoken,
The daily thoughts of labour and sorrow slumber
At the sight of the beauty that greets them, for the charm
                  they have broken.

## So sweet love seemed

*A charming, musical lyric which Bridges included in his collection of* Shorter Poems *in 1890.*

So sweet love seemed that April morn,
When first we kissed beside the thorn,
So strangely sweet, it was not strange
We thought that love could never change.

But I can tell—let truth be told—
That love will change in growing old ;
Though day by day is nought to see,
So delicate his motions be.

And in the end 'twill come to pass
Quite to forget what once he was,
Nor even in fancy to recall
The pleasure that was all in all.

His little spring, that sweet we found,
So deep in summer floods is drowned,
I wonder, bathed in joy complete,
How love so young could be so sweet.

## Nightingales

*In this ode, as in much of his poetry, Bridges celebrates the pure and the beautiful.*

Beautiful must be the mountains whence ye come,
And bright in the fruitful valleys the streams, wherefrom
Ye learn your song :
Where are those starry woods ? O might I wander there,
Among the flowers, which in that heavenly air
Bloom the year long !

Nay, barren are those mountains and spent the streams :
Our song is the voice of desire, that haunts our dreams,
A throe of the heart,
Whose pining visions dim, forbidden hopes profound,
No dying cadence nor long sigh can sound,
For all our art.

Alone, aloud in the raptured ear of men
We pour our dark nocturnal secret ; and then,
As night is withdrawn
From these sweet-springing meads and bursting boughs of May,
Dream, while the innumerable choir of day
Welcome the dawn.

## When Death to either shall come

*Bridges was particularly fond of writing words for music. This poem is reminiscent of the lyrics written by Campion and the poet-musicians of the seventeenth century.*

When Death to either shall come,—
    I pray it be first to me,—
Be happy as ever at home,
    If so, as I wish, it be.

Possess thy heart, my own ;
    And sing to the child on thy knee,
Or read to thyself alone
    The songs that I made for thee.

## Noel : Christmas Eve, 1913
### Pax hominibus bonae voluntatis

*One of Bridges's laureate poems, subtitled "peace to men of good will", and greatly appreciated by King George V.*

A frosty Christmas Eve
    when the stars were shining
Fared I forth alone
    where westward falls the hill,
And from many a village
    in the water'd valley

Distant music reach'd me
    peals of bells arising :
The constellated sounds
    ran sprinkling on earth's floor
As the dark vault above
    with stars was spangled o'er.

Then sped my thought to keep
    that first Christmas of all
When the shepherds watching
    by their folds ere the dawn
Heard music in the fields
    and marveling could not tell
Whether it were angels
    or the bright stars singing.

Now blessed be the tow'rs
    that crown England so fair
That stand up strong in prayer
    unto God for our souls :
Blessed be their founders
    (said I) an' our country folk
Who are ringing for Christ
    in the belfries to-night
With arms lifted to clutch
    the rattling ropes that race
Into the dark above
    and the mad romping din.

But to me heard afar
   it was starry music
Angels' song, comforting
   as the comfort of Christ
When he spake tenderly
   to his sorrowful flock :
The old words came to me
   by the riches of time
Mellow'd and transfigured
   as I stood on the hill
Heark'ning in the aspect
   of th' eternal silence.

## Fortunatus Nimium

*Bridges took the title for this poem from Virgil's* Georgics. *It means "too happy" or "happy beyond bearing", an unusual perspective in such troubled times.*

I have lain in the sun
I have toil'd as I might
I have thought as I would
And now it is night.

My bed full of sleep
My heart of content
For friends that I met
The way that I went.

I welcome fatigue
While frenzy and care
Like thin summer clouds
Go melting in air.

To dream as I may
And awake when I will
With the song of the birds
And the sun on the hill.

Or death—were it death—
To what should I wake
Who loved in my home
All life for its sake ?

What good have I wrought ?
I laugh to have learned
That joy cannot come
Unless it be earned ;

For a happier lot
Than God giveth me
It never hath been
Nor ever shall be.

# John Masefield

1878–1967

When John Betjeman met Masefield at a poetry reading in 1923, he was surprised to find a spare, quiet, man with luminous blue eyes instead of the breezy sea-salt which the poetry had led him to expect.

Masefield described his early childhood years in Herefordshire as having been spent in paradise, but his parents' early deaths delivered him into the care of unimaginative and unsympathetic guardians. At the age of thirteen he was sent to train as a merchant seaman. He loved the sea and ships, but he suffered badly from seasickness and he hated the violence of the seaman's life. He jumped ship in New York and worked in factories and bars, all the time reading and growing more determined to be a writer.

He returned to England to work as a bank clerk but, encouraged by meeting W. B. Yeats, Laurence Binyon and J. M. Synge, he left the bank to write full-time. His first book of poems, *Salt-Water Ballads* (which included "I must down to the sea again"), was a success. But Masefield was often in poor health and he had to work very hard to earn enough. Often journalism would crowd out poetry. He persevered and by 1923, when Betjeman met him, he was an established and popular poet. His *Collected Poems* would sell around 200,000 copies.

When Austin died in 1913 Masefield was considered as a possible successor, but he had to wait until the death of Bridges in 1930 before he was offered the poet laureateship. Ramsay Mac-Donald, the first Labour Prime Minister, chose a man known for his affinity with ordinary people, with little formal education, whose own life had been a struggle. Masefield was poet laureate for thirty-seven years, longer than all his predecessors except Tennyson. He took the job very seriously, producing many odes, duly published in *The Times*. His best days as a writer were over, but he continued working. At his death he left fifty books of verse, twenty novels and eight plays. He was an active promoter of poetry and other poets ; a man who may have brought little charisma and excitement to the post, but one with admirable persistence, courage and energy.

# Trade Winds

*One of the poems of ships and the sea from Masefield's first book,* Salt-Water Ballads.

In the harbour, in the island, in the Spanish Seas,
Are the tiny white houses and the orange-trees,
And day-long, night-long, the cool and pleasant breeze
 Of the steady Trade Winds blowing.

There is the red wine, the nutty Spanish ale,
The shuffle of the dancers, the old salt's tale,
The squeaking fiddle, and the soughing in the sail
 Of the steady Trade Winds blowing.

And o'nights there 's fire-flies and the yellow moon,
And in the ghostly palm-trees the sleepy tune
Of the quiet voice calling me, the long low croon
 Of the steady Trade Winds blowing.

# Sea-Fever

*Masefield's best-known and best-loved poem is full of his feeling for the sea.*

I must down to the seas again, to the lonely sea and the sky,
And all I ask is a tall ship and a star to steer her by,
And the wheel's kick and the wind's song and the white sail's
          shaking,
And a grey mist on the sea's face and a grey dawn breaking.

I must down to the seas again, for the call of the running tide
Is a wild call and a clear call that may not be denied ;
And all I ask is a windy day with the white clouds flying,
And the flung spray and the blown spume, and the sea-gulls
crying.

I must down to the seas again, to the vagrant gypsy life,
To the gull's way and the whale's way where the wind 's like
a whetted knife ;
And all I ask is a merry yarn from a laughing fellow-rover,
And quiet sleep and a sweet dream when the long trick 's
over.


## Cargoes

*Another of Masefield's sea poems, in which romance makes way for more mundane reality.*

Quinquireme of Nineveh from distant Ophir
Rowing home to haven in sunny Palestine,
With a cargo of ivory,
And apes and peacocks,
Sandalwood, cedarwood, and sweet white wine.

Stately Spanish galleon coming from the Isthmus,
Dipping through the Tropics by the palm-green shores,
With a cargo of diamonds,
Emeralds, amethysts,
Topazes, and cinnamon, and gold moidores.

Dirty British coaster with a salt-caked smoke stack
Butting through the Channel in the mad March days,
With a cargo of Tyne coal,
Road-rail, pig-lead,
Firewood, iron-ware, and cheap tin trays.

## The Emigrant

*A sailor's song, full of the irresistible call of the sea.*

Going by Daly's shanty I heard the boys within
Dancing the Spanish hornpipe to Driscoll's violin,
I heard the sea-boots shaking the rough planks of the floor,
But I was going westward, I hadn't heart for more.

All down the windy village the noise rang in my ears,
Old sea-boots stamping, shuffling, it brought the bitter teas,
The old tune piped and quavered, the lilts came clear and
                strong,
But I was going westward, I couldn't join the song.

There were the grey stone houses, the night wind blowing
keen,
The hill-sides pale with moonlight, the young corn springing
                green,
The hearth nooks lit and kindly, with dear friends good to see,
But I was going westward, and the ship waited for me.

# The Seekers

*A poem from Masefield's collection* Ballads and Poems, *published in 1910.*

Friends and loves we have none, nor wealth nor blessed abode,
But the hope of the City of God at the other end of the road.

Not for us are content, and quiet, and peace of mind,
For we go seeking a city that we shall never find.

There is no solace on earth for us—for such as we—
Who search for a hidden city that we shall never see.

Only the road and the dawn, the sun, the wind, and the rain,
And the watch fire under stars, and sleep, and the road again.

We seek the City of God, and the haunt where beauty dwells,
And we find the noisy mart and the sound of burial bells.

Never the golden city, where radiant people meet,
But the dolorous town where mourners are going about the
        street.

We travel the dusty road till the light of the day is dim,
And sunset shows us spires away on the world's rim.

We travel from dawn to dusk, till the day is past and by,
Seeking the Holy City beyond the rim of the sky.

Friends and loves we have none, nor wealth nor blest abode,
But the hope of the City of God at the other end of the road.

# The West Wind

*This poem expresses the strong pull towards home felt by the traveller.*

It 's a warm wind, the west wind, full of birds' cries ;
I never hear the west wind but tears are in my eyes.
For it comes from the west lands, the old brown hills,
And April 's in the west wind, and daffodils.

It 's a fine land, the west land, for hearts as tired as mine,
Apple orchards blossom there, and the air 's like wine.
There is cool green grass there, where men may lie at rest,
And the thrushes are in song there, fluting from the nest.

"Will ye not come home, brother ? ye have been long away,
It 's April, and blossom time, and white is the may :
And bright is the sun, brother, and warm is the rain,—
Will yet not come home, brother, home to us again ?

"The young corn is green, brother, where the rabbits run,
It 's blue sky, and white clouds, and warm rain and sun.
It 's song to a man's soul, brother, fire to a man's brain,
To hear the wild bees and see the merry spring again.

"Larks are singing in the west, brother, above the green wheat,
So will ye not come home, brother, and rest your tired feet ?
I've a balm for bruised hearts, brother, sleep for aching eyes,"
Says the warm wind, the west wind, full of birds' cries.

It 's the white road westwards is the road I must tread
To the green grass, the cool grass, and rest for heart and head,
To the violets and the warm hearts and the thrushes' song,
In the fine land, the west land, the land where I belong.

# Night is on the downland, on the lonely moorland,

*A meditation on the English countryside, which Masefield wrote during the First World War.*

Night is on the downland, on the lonely moorland,
On the hills where the wind goes over sheep-bitten turf,
Where the bent grass beats upon the unploughed poorland
And the pine-woods roar like the surf.

Here the Roman lived on the wind-barren lonely,
Dark now and haunted by the moorland fowl ;
None comes here now but the peewit only,
And moth-like death in the owl.

Beauty was here, on this beetle-droning downland ;
The thought of a Cæsar in the purple came
From the palace by the Tiber in the Roman townland
To this wind-swept hill with no name.

Lonely Beauty came here and was here in sadness,
Brave as a thought on the frontier of the mind,
In the camp of the wild upon the march of madness,
The bright-eyed Queen of the Blind.

Now where Beauty was are the wind-withered gorses,
Moaning like old men in the hill-wind's blast ;
The flying sky is dark with the running horses,
And the night is full of the past.

## The Rider at the Gate

*One of the great ballads for which Masefield is so admired.*

A windy night was blowing on Rome,
The cressets guttered on Cæsar's home,
The fish-boats, moored at the bridge, were breaking
The rush of the river to yellow foam.

The hinges whined to the shutters shaking,
When clip-clop-clep came a horse-hoof raking
The stones of the road at Cæsar's gate ;
The spear-butts jarred at the guard's awaking.

"Who goes there ?" said the guard at the gate.
"What is the news, that you ride so late ?"
"News most pressing, that must be spoken
To Cæsar alone, and that cannot wait."

"The Cæsar sleeps ; you must show a token
That the news suffice that he be awoken.
What is the news, and whence do you come ?
For no light cause may his sleep be broken."

"Out of the dark of the sands I come,
From the dark of death, with news for Rome.
A word so fell that it must be uttered
Though it strike the soul of the Cæsar dumb."

*Cæsar turned in his bed and muttered,*
*With a struggle for breath the lamp-flame guttered ;*
*Calpurnia heard her husband moan :*
   *"The house is falling,*
*The beaten men come into their own."*

"Speak your word," said the guard at the gate ;
"Yes, but bear it to Cæsar straight,
Say, 'Your murderer's knives are honing,
Your killer's gang is lying in wait.'

"Out of the wind that is blowing and moaning,
Through the city palace and the country loaning,
I cry, 'For the world's sake, Cæsar, beware,
And take this warning as my atoning.

" 'Beware of the Court, of the palace stair,
Of the downcast friend who speaks so fair,
Keep from the Senate, for Death is going
On many men's feet to meet you there.'

"I, who am dead, have ways of knowing
Of the crop of death that the quick are sowing.
I, who was Pompey, cry it aloud
From the dark of death, from the wind blowing.

"I, who was Pompey, once was proud,
Now I lie in the sand without a shroud ;
I cry to Cæsar out of my pain,
'Cæsar, beware, your death is vowed.' "

The light grew grey on the window-pane,
The windcocks swung in a burst of rain,
The window of Cæsar flung unshuttered,
The horse-hoofs died into wind again.

*Cæsar turned in his bed and muttered,*
*With a struggle for breath the lamp-flame guttered;*
*Calpurnia heard her husband moan:*
*    "The house is falling,*
*The beaten men come into their own."*

# Cecil Day Lewis

1904–1972

Although not the best poet of his generation, Cecil Day Lewis was one of the best known. He had come to the fore in the 1930s with W. H. Auden and Stephen Spender, one of a group of young writers determined to make the world a better place, to reform and not simply to record it. By 1967, when he became poet laureate, he had published several volumes of verse ; he had been Professor of Poetry at Oxford ; he was often on the radio or on television ; anthologies he had compiled were used in schools and the detective stories he wrote under the name Nicholas Blake attracted a large following.

Day Lewis was Anglo-Irish. His mother's death, when he was only four, and the difficult and distant relationship he had with his clergyman father, marked him strongly. He was by nature contradictory and paradoxical. His son Sean would describe him as a "poet of the divided mind and the divided heart". Cecil Day Lewis believed that it was from these divisions that his poetry sprang.

While a student at Oxford, he joined the young men gathered around Auden. He was the longest, most committed Communist of this group, although he was a party member for only two years. He had little real talent for, or insight into, politics. He worked for some time as a schoolteacher before becoming a full-time writer and moving with his family to Devon. A romantic richness and melancholy pastoral characterize his writing. Often his poetry has the very attractive quality of reverie.

During the Second World War Day Lewis joined the Home Guard and worked for the Ministry of Information. His emotional life was always fairly turbulent, yet, as he grew older, he became something of an establishment figure. The contrast with his radical youth was not lost on his critics. He was a conscientious poet laureate, but for only six years, years when he was often very ill. Competitive by nature, he enjoyed the honour which had been bestowed on him. Asked if he was glad to be the laureate he replied, "Certainly, it's a feather in my cap ; we Irish like feathers in our caps."

# The Conflict

*Day Lewis valued only two of the political poems he wrote—this was one, even though it is a poem that shows him to be very much undecided, with what his son Sean would call "a divided mind".*

I sang as one
Who on a tilting deck sings
To keep men's courage up, though the wave hangs
That shall cut off their sun.

As storm-cocks sing,
Flinging their natural answer in the wind's teeth,
And care not if it is waste of breath
Or birth-carol of spring.

As ocean-flyer clings
To height, to the last drop of spirit driving on
While yet ahead is land to be won
And work for wings.

Singing I was at peace,
Above the clouds, outside the ring:
For sorrow finds a swift release in song
And pride its poise.

Yet living here,
As one between two massing powers I live
Whom neutrality cannot save
Nor occupation cheer.

None such shall be left alive :
The innocent wing is soon shot down,
And private stars fade in the blood-red dawn
Where two worlds strive.

The red advance of life
Contracts pride, calls out the common blood,
Beats song into a single blade,
Makes a depth-charge of grief.

Move then with new desires,
For where we used to build and love
Is no man's land, and only ghosts can live
Between two fires.

## A Carol

*Another of Day Lewis's poems from the 1930s, a time for him of great political involvement and commitment.*

Oh hush thee, my baby,
Thy cradle's in pawn :
No blankets to cover thee
Cold and forlorn.
The stars in the bright sky
Look down and are dumb
At the heir of the ages
Asleep in a slum.

The hooters are blowing,
No heed let him take ;
When baby is hungry
'Tis best not to wake.
Thy mother is crying,
Thy dad's on the dole :
Two shillings a week is
The price of a soul.

## Departure in the Dark

*This poems treats one of Day Lewis's most common themes—parting,
change, impermanence.*

Nothing so sharply reminds a man he is mortal
As leaving a place
In a winter morning's dark, the air on his face
Unkind as the touch of sweating metal :
Simple goodbyes to children or friends become
A felon's numb
Farewell, and love that was a warm, a meeting place—
Love is the suicide's grave under the nettles.

Gloomed and clemmed as if by an imminent ice-age
Lies the dear world
Of your street-strolling, field-faring.  The senses, curled
At the dead end of a shrinking passage,
Care not if close the inveterate hunters creep,
And memories sleep
Like mammoths in lost caves.  Drear, extinct is the world,
And has no voice for consolation or presage.

There is always something at such times of the passover,
When the dazed heart
Beats for it knows not what, whether you part
From home or prison, acquaintance or lover—
Something wrong with the time-table, something unreal
In the scrambled meal
And the bag ready packed by the door, as though the heart
Has gone ahead, or is staying here for ever.

No doubt for the Israelites that early morning
It was hard to be sure
If home were prison or prison home :  the desire
Going forth meets the desire returning.
This land, that had cut their pride down to the bone
Was now their own
By ancient deeds of sorrow.  Beyond, there was nothing
          sure
But a desert of freedom to quench their fugitive yearnings.

At this blind hour the heart is informed of nature's
Ruling that man
Should be nowhere a more tenacious settler than
Among wry thorns and ruins, yet nurture
A seed of discontent in his ripest ease.
There's a kind of release
And a kind of torment in every goodbye for every man
And will be, even to the last of his dark departures.

# Hornpipe

*Day Lewis loved music and had a very pleasing singing voice. This poem is redolent of the hornpipe, a dance in 4/4 time usually associated with sailors.*

Now the peak of summer's past, the sky is overcast
And the love we swore would last for an age seems deceit :
Paler is the guelder since the day we first beheld her
In blush beside the elder drifting sweet, drifting sweet.

Oh quickly they fade—the sunny esplanade,
Speed-boats, wooden spades, and the dunes where we've
          lain :
Others will be lying amid the sea-pinks sighing
For love to be undying, and they'll sigh in vain.

It's hurrah for each night we have spent our love so lightly
And never dreamed there might be no more to spend at all.
It's goodbye to every lover who thinks he'll live in clover
All his life, for noon is over soon and night-dews fall.

If I could keep you there with the berries in your hair
And your lacy fingers fair as the may, sweet may,
I'd have no heart to do it, for to stay love is to rue it
And the harder we pursue it, the faster it's away.

# If love means exploration

*This sonnet is part of one of Day Lewis's longer poems, "Moods of Love".*

If love means exploration—the divine
Growth of a new discoverer first conceived
In flesh, only the stranger can be loved :
Familiar loving grooves its own decline.

If change alone is true—the ever-shifting
Base of each real or illusive show,
Inconstancy's a law :  the you that now
Loves her, to otherness is blindly drifting.

But chance and fretting time and your love change her
Subtly from year to year, from known to new :
So she will always be the elusive stranger,
If you can hold her present self in view.

Find here, in constant change, faithful perceiving,
The paradox and mode of all true loving.

## Circus Lion

*Published in the 1962 collection* The Gate.

Lumbering haunches, pussyfoot tread, a pride of
Lions under the arcs
Walk in, leap up, sit pedestalled there and glum
As a row of Dickensian clerks.

Their eyes are slag.  Only a muscle flickering,
A bored, theatrical roar
Witness now to the furnaces that drove them
Exultant along the spoor.

In preyward, elastic leap they are sent through paper
Hoops at another's will
After a whip's crack :  afterwards, in their cages,
They tear the provided kill.

Caught young, can this public animal ever dream of
Stars, distances and thunders ?
Does he twitch in sleep for ticks, dried water-holes,
Rogue elephants, or hunters ?

Sawdust, not burning desert, is the ground
Of his to-fro, to-fro pacing,
Barred with the zebra shadows that imply
Sun's free wheel, man's coercing.

See this abdicated beast, once king
Of them all, nibble his claws :
Not anger enough left—no, nor despair—
To break his teeth on the bars.

# Walking Away

*Day Lewis wrote this poem for his first son, Sean.*

It is eighteen years ago, almost to the day—
A sunny day with the leaves just turning,
The touch-lines new-ruled—since I watched you play
Your first game of football, then, like a satellite
Wrenched from its orbit, go drifting away

Behind a scatter of boys.  I can see
You walking away from me towards the school
With the pathos of a half-fledged thing set free
Into a wilderness, the gait of one
Who finds no path where the path should be.

That hesitant figure, eddying away
Like a winged seed loosened from its parent stem,
Has something I never quite grasp to convey
About nature's give-and-take—the small, the scorching
Ordeals which fire one's irresolute clay.

I have had worse partings, but none that so
Gnaws at my mind still.  Perhaps it is roughly
Saying what God alone could perfectly show—
How selfhood begins with a walking away,
And love is proved in the letting go.

## *from* Battle of Britain

*The first two verses from one of Day Lewis's official laureate poems,*
*written for the premiere of a film about the battle between the British and*
*German air forces in 1940.*

What did we earth-bound make of it ?  A tangle
Of vapour trails, a vertiginously high
Swarming of midges, at most a fiery angel
Hurled out of heaven, was all we could descry.

How could we know the agony and pride
That scrawled those fading signatures up there,
And the cool expertise of them who died
Or lived through that delirium of the air ?

## Where are the War Poets ?

*Written in the early years of the Second World War.*

They who in folly or mere greed
Enslaved religion, markets, laws,
Borrow our language now and bid
Us to speak up in freedom's cause.

It is the logic of our times,
No subject for immortal verse—
That we who lived by honest dreams
Defend the bad against the worse.

# SIR JOHN BETJEMAN

## 1906–1984

John Betjeman was appointed poet laureate on the death of Cecil Day Lewis in 1972. "Lucky old England to have him," wrote his friend and fellow-poet Philip Larkin. Betjeman was already the best-known and most loved poet of his generation. His witty, comic verse had a very wide appeal, reaching far beyond traditional poetry readers. Winner of the Queen's Gold Medal for Poetry in 1960 and knighted in 1969, he was the poet of cosy suburbs and garden gnomes, of railways and churches, of England's countryside and provincial towns.

Betjeman was born in Highgate, north London. He was an only child and often felt lonely and insecure, feelings intensified by his father's deafness and his mother's unthinking chatter. He took comfort in his teddy bear, Archibald, who remained with him all his life. He was taught briefly at Highgate School by T. S. Eliot before going on to Marlborough, which he disliked, and then to Oxford where he made many friends and acquaintances, among them W. H. Auden and Louis MacNeice. A bon viveur and aesthete, he left the university without a degree. Determined not to enter the family business, at first he made his living from schoolmastering and journalism. His first book of poems was published in 1931; his *Collected Poems*, which appeared in 1958, was particularly well received, as was *Summoned by Bells*, a long autobiographical poem which looked back to Wordsworth's *Prelude*.

Betjeman was happy to accept the laureateship, pleased to follow in the footsteps of Tennyson, one of his heroes. He asked that the traditional payment in drink, by now in abeyance, should be reinstated and he enjoyed sharing with his friends the wine and champagne sent by the Queen's wine merchant. But he found it difficult to write poems for particular occasions—Princess Anne's wedding in 1973, the Queen's Silver Jubilee in 1976. He worried that he would let his public down. In the last six years of his life, in increasingly poor health, he wrote very little. Yet at his death in 1984 his reputation remained high—popular poet, broadcaster, social historian, railway enthusiast, conservationist, humorist, very loveable Englishman.

# Slough

*This poem, a typical mix of lightness and seriousness, was first published in 1937.*

Come, friendly bombs, and fall on Slough
It isn't fit for humans now,
There isn't grass to graze a cow
  Swarm over, Death !

Come, bombs, and blow to smithereens
Those air-conditioned, bright canteens,
Tinned fruit, tinned meat, tinned milk, tinned beans
  Tinned minds, tinned breath.

Mess up the mess they call a town—
A house for ninety-seven down
And once a week a half-a-crown
  For twenty years,

And get that man with double chin
Who'll always cheat and always win,
Who washes his repulsive skin
  In women's tears,

And smash his desk of polished oak
And smash his hands so used to stroke
And stop his boring dirty joke
  And make him yell.

But spare the bald young clerks who add
The profits of the stinking cad ;
It's not their fault that they are made,
    They've tasted Hell.

It's not their fault they do not know
The birdsong from the radio,
It's not their fault they often go
    To Maidenhead

And talk of sports and makes of cars
In various bogus Tudor bars
And daren't look up and see the stars
    But belch instead.

In labour-saving homes, with care
Their wives frizz out peroxide hair
And dry it in synthetic air
    And paint their nails.

Come, friendly bombs, and fall on Slough
To get it ready for the plough.
The cabbages are coming now ;
    The earth exhales.

# In Westminster Abbey

*First published in 1940, in the early months of the war.*

Let me take this other glove off
  As the *vox humana* swells,
And the beauteous fields of Eden
  Bask beneath the Abbey bells.
Here, where England's statesmen lie,
Listen to a lady's cry.

Gracious Lord, oh bomb the Germans.
  Spare their women for Thy Sake,
And if that is not too easy
  We will pardon Thy Mistake.
But, gracious Lord, whate'er shall be,
Don't let anyone bomb me.

Keep our Empire undismembered
  Guide our Forces by Thy Hand,
Gallant blacks from far Jamaica,
  Honduras and Togoland ;
Protect them Lord in all their fights
And, even more, protect the whites.

Think of what our Nation stands for,
  Books from Boots' and country lanes,
Free speech, free passes, class distinction,
  Democracy and proper drains.
Lord, put beneath Thy special care
One-eighty-nine Cadogan Square.

Although dear Lord I am a sinner,
   I have done no major crime ;
Now I'll come to Evening Service
   Whensoever I have the time.
So, Lord, reserve for me a crown,
And do not let my shares go down.

I will labour for Thy Kingdom,
   Help our lads to win the war,
Send white feathers to the cowards
   Join the Women's Army Corps,
Then wash the Steps around Thy Throne
In the Eternal Safety Zone.

Now I feel a little better,
   What a treat to hear Thy Word,
Where the bones of leading statesmen,
   Have so often been interr'd.
And now, dear Lord, I cannot wait
Because I have a luncheon date.

## A Shropshire Lad

*Captain Matthew Webb, a Shropshire man, in 1875 became the first person to swim the Channel. He tried again for immortality by swimming across the rapids at the head of the Niagara Falls but this time he failed and was drowned.*

The gas was on in the Institute,
    The flare was up in the gym,
A man was running a mineral line,
    A lass was singing a hymn,
When Captain Webb the Dawley man,
    Captain Webb from Dawley,
Came swimming along in the old canal
    That carried the bricks to Lawley.
        Swimming along—
        Swimming along—
        Swimming along from Severn,
And paying a call at Dawley Bank while swimming
            along to Heaven.

The sun shone low on the railway line
    And over the bricks and stacks,
And in at the upstairs windows
    Of the Dawley houses' backs,
When we saw the ghost of Captain Webb,
    Webb in a water sheeting,
Come dripping along in a bathing dress
    To the Saturday evening meeting.

Dripping along—
Dripping along—
To the Congregational Hall ;
Dripping and still he rose over the sill and faded
away in a wall.

There wasn't a man in Oakengates
That hadn't got hold of the tale,
And over the valley in Ironbridge,
And round by Coalbrookdale,
How Captain Webb the Dawley man,
Captain Webb from Dawley,
Rose rigid and dead from the old canal
That carries the bricks to Lawley.
Rigid and dead—
Rigid and dead—
To the Saturday congregation,
Paying a call at Dawley Bank on his way to his
destination.

## In a Bath Teashop

*Betjeman said that he was happiest when writing poetry, which he thought of as "the putting down of moments of ecstasy or depression in as short a way as possible".*

"Let us not speak, for the love we bear one another—
    Let us hold hands and look."
She, such a very ordinary little woman ;
    He, such a thumping crook ;
But both, for a moment, little lower than the angels
    In the teashop's ingle-nook.

## Sun and Fun
### Song of a night-club proprietress

*Betjeman is famous for his wonderful, funny portraits of young women, but he was also able to sympathize with older women, often not particularly attractive ones.*

I walked into the night-club in the morning ;
    There was kummel on the handle of the door.
The ashtrays were unemptied,
The cleaning unattempted,
    And a squashed tomato sandwich on the floor.

I pulled aside the thick magenta curtains
    —So Regency, so Regency, my dear—
And a host of little spiders

Ran a race across the ciders
    To a box of baby 'pollies by the beer.

Oh sun upon the summer-going by-pass
    Where ev'rything is speeding to the sea,
And wonder beyond wonder
That here where lorries thunder
    The sun should ever percolate to me.

When Boris used to call in his Sedanca,
    When Teddy took me down to his estate
When my nose excited passion,
When my clothes were in the fashion,
    When my beaux were never cross if I was late,

There was sun enough for lazing upon beaches,
    There was fun enough for far into the night.
But I'm dying now and done for,
What on earth was all the fun for?
    For I'm old and ill and terrified and tight.

## How to Get On in Society

*Published in 1954—an irresistible mix of affection and satire.*

Phone for the fish-knives, Norman
    As Cook is a little unnerved ;
You kiddies have crumpled the serviettes
    And I must have things daintily served.

Are the requisites all in the toilet ?
    The frills round the cutlets can wait
Till the girl has replenished the cruets
    And switched on the logs in the grate.

It's ever so close in the lounge, dear,
    But the vestibule's comfy for tea
And Howard is out riding on horseback
    So do come and take some with me.

Now here is a fork for your pastries
    And do use the couch for your feet ;
I know what I wanted to ask you—
    Is trifle sufficient for sweet ?

Milk and then just as it comes dear ?
    I'm afraid the preserve's full of stones ;
Beg pardon, I'm soiling the doileys
    With afternoon tea-cakes and scones.

## Late-Flowering Lust

*A sense of mortality and deep sadness creeps into some of Betjeman's later poems.*

My head is bald, my breath is bad,
    Unshaven is my chin,
I have not now the joys I had
    When I was young in sin.

I run my fingers down your dress
    With brandy-certain aim
And you respond to my caress
    And maybe feel the same.

But I've a picture of my own
    On this reunion night,
Wherein two skeletons are shewn
    To hold each other tight ;

Dark sockets look on emptiness
    Which once was loving-eyed,
The mouth that opens for a kiss
    Has got no tongue inside.

I cling to you inflamed with fear
    As now you cling to me,
I feel how frail you are my dear
    And wonder what will be—

A week ? or twenty years remain ?
   And then—what kind of death ?
A losing fight with frightful pain
   Or a gasping fight for breath ?

Too long we let our bodies cling,
   We cannot hide disgust
At all the thoughts that in us spring
   From this late-flowering lust.

# Ted Hughes

1930–1998

Ted Hughes's unexpected death late in 1998 was greeted with disbelief and shock. Since the publication in 1957 of his first collection of poems, *The Hawk in the Rain*, he had been a powerful presence, a fixed landmark in English poetry. It was, wrote a fellow poet, as if a giant oak had toppled, leaving only saplings below.

Hughes was born in West Yorkshire. After National Service in the RAF he went to Cambridge where he met the young American poet Sylvia Plath. They married in 1956. In February 1963, estranged from her husband, Plath killed herself. Hughes wrote poetry for three years. For thirty-five years he refused to talk about his marriage and its aftermath. His critics charged him with Plath's death and with suppressing her writing. He answered them fully and brilliantly in *Birthday Letters*, a sequence of autobiographical poems published nine months before he died.

Hughes's poems are always intense, often fierce, even ferocious. His genius was for the inner life of landscape, animals, plants, for the struggle between opposing forms, the struggle in the soil as well as in the soul. With *Crow*, a sequence of poems published in 1970, he introduced the symbol of the predatory, mocking, indestructible crow through which he retold the legends of creation and birth. His translation *Tales from Ovid*, myths of love gone wrong, of bodies tragically transformed, was acclaimed when it appeared in 1997. He wrote some fine poetry and plays for children. His mythical story, *The Iron Man*, is already a children's classic.

Hughes was appointed poet laureate on John Betjeman's death in 1984. He did not attempt to redefine the laureateship, but with his instinct for harmony and wholeness, his unswerving truth to his own sense of the world, his conviction of the essential link between the well being of the country and of its poets, he raised its status and greatly enhanced its reputation.

---

## The Thought-Fox

*This is Ted Hughes's first animal poem. He wrote it one snowy night in London. Hughes said himself that the poem doesn't have anything that can easily be called a meaning. It's about a fox which is both a fox and not a fox, both a fox and a spirit. "It is very real to me... The words have made a body for it and given it somewhere to walk."*

I imagine this midnight moment's forest :
Something else is alive
Beside the clock's loneliness
And this blank page where my fingers move.

Through the window I see no star :
Something more near
Though deeper within darkness
Is entering the loneliness :

Cold, delicately as the dark snow
A fox's nose touches twig, leaf ;
Two eyes serve a movement, that now
And again now, and now, and now

Sets neat prints into the snow
Between trees, and warily a lame
Shadow lags by stump and in hollow
Of a body that is bold to come

Across clearings, an eye,
A widening deepening greenness,
Brilliantly, concentratedly,
Coming about its own business

Till, with a sudden sharp hot stink of fox
It enters the dark hole of the head.
The window is starless still ;  the clock ticks,
The page is printed.

## Fern

*From Ted Hughes's book* Wodwo *published in 1967.*

Here is the fern's frond, unfurling a gesture,
Like a conductor whose music will now be pause
And the one note of silence
To which the whole earth dances gravely.

The mouse's ear unfurls its trust,
The spider takes up her bequest,
And the retina
Reins the creation with a bridle of water.

And, among them, the fern
Dances gravely, like the plume
Of a warrior returning, under the low hills,

Into his own kingdom.

# Pibroch

*The pibroch is a kind of bagpipe music, a set of variations on a theme.*
*The effect produced, both by the music and by this poem, is of variations*
*on a lament or dirge.*

The sea cries with its meaningless voice
Treating alike its dead and its living,
Probably bored with the appearance of heaven
After so many millions of nights without sleep,
Without purpose, without self-deception.

Stone likewise.  A pebble is imprisoned
Like nothing in the Universe.
Created for black sleep.  Or growing
Conscious of the sun's red spot occasionally,
Then dreaming it is the foetus of God.

Over the stone rushes the wind
Able to mingle with nothing,
Like the hearing of the blind stone itself.
Or turns, as if the stone's mind came feeling
A fantasy of directions.

Drinking the sea and eating the rock
A tree struggles to make leaves—
An old woman fallen from space
Unprepared for these conditions.
She hangs on, because her mind's gone completely.

Minute after minute, aeon after aeon,
Nothing lets up or develops.
And this is neither a bad variant nor a tryout.
This is where the staring angels go through.
This is where all the stars bow down.

*The next three poems are from* Crow, *published in 1970.* Crow *is a force,
an accident of God, the bare bones of a myth.  Hughes uses Crow as a
way of unlocking and confronting something very personal, something
restraining and restricting him, a half-conscious taboo.*

## Crow's Fall

When Crow was white he decided the sun was too white.
He decided it glared much too whitely.
He decided to attack it and defeat it.

He got his strength flush and in full glitter.
He clawed and fluffed his rage up.
He aimed his beak direct at the sun's centre.

He laughed himself to the centre of himself

And attacked.

At his battle cry trees grew suddenly old,
Shadows flattened.

But the sun brightened—
It brightened, and Crow returned charred black.

He opened his mouth but what came out was charred black.

"Up there," he managed,
"Where white is black and black is white, I won."

## Crow's Vanity

Looking close in the evil mirror Crow saw
Mistings of civilizations    towers    gardens
Battles he wiped the glass    but there came

Mistings of skyscrapers    webs of cities
Steaming the glass he wiped it    there came

Spread of swampferns fronded on the mistings
A trickling spider    he wiped the glass    he peered

For a glimpse of the usual grinning face

But it was no good he was breathing too heavy
And too hot    and space was too cold

And here came the misty ballerinas
The burning gulfs    the hanging gardens    it was eerie

## Conjuring in Heaven

So finally there was nothing.
It was put inside nothing.
Nothing was added to it
And to prove it didn't exist
Squashed flat as nothing with nothing.

Chopped up with a nothing
Shaken in a nothing
Turned completely inside out
And scattered over nothing—
So everybody saw that it was nothing
And that nothing more could be done with it

And so it was dropped.  Prolonged applause in Heaven.

It hit the ground and broke open—

There lay Crow, cataleptic.

# A March Calf

*This poem is from the collection* Season Songs, *published in 1976, and comes from Hughes's life in Devon, working alongside his father-in-law on his farm.*

Right from the start he is dressed in his best—his blacks
        and his whites
Little Fauntleroy—quiffed and glossy,
A Sunday suit, a wedding natty get-up,
Standing in dunged straw

Under cobwebby beams, near the mud wall,
Half of him legs,
Shining-eyed, requiring nothing more
But that mother's milk come back often.

Everything else is in order, just as it is.
Let the summer skies hold off, for the moment.
This is just as he wants it.
A little at a time, of each new thing, is best.

Too much and too sudden is too frightening—
When I block the light, a bulk from space,
To let him in to his mother for a suck,
He bolts a yard or two, then freezes,

Staring from every hair in all directions,
Ready for the worst, shut up in his hopeful religion,
A little syllogism
With a wet blue-reddish muzzle, for God's thumb.

You see all his hopes bustling
As he reaches between the worn rails towards
The topheavy oven of his mother.
He trembles to grow, stretching his curl-tip tongue—

What did cattle ever find here
To make this dear little fellow
So eager to prepare himself?
He is already in the race, and quivering to win—

His new purpled eyeball swivel-jerks
In the elbowing push of his plans.
Hungry people are getting hungrier,
Butchers developing expertise and markets,

But he just wobbles his tail—and glistens
Within his dapper profile
Unaware of how his whole lineage
Has been tied up.

He shivers for feel of the world licking his side.
He is like an ember—one glow
Of lighting himself up
With the fuel of himself, breathing and brightening.

Soon he'll plunge out, to scatter his seething joy,
To be present at the grass,
To be free on the surface of such a wideness,
To find himself himself. To stand. To moo.

## Little Salmon Hymn

*One of two poems written for the Queen Mother and published in 1985.*
*Hughes explained that, because the Queen Mother was patron of the*
*Salmon and Trout Association, she is the godmother of the salmon itself.*

Between the sea's hollows and inland hills,
Naked as at birth
The salmon slips, a simple shuttle
Clothing the earth.

Say the constellations are flocks.  And the sea-dawns,
Collecting colour, give it,
The sea-spray the spectrum.  Salmon find
The fibre and weave it.

Salmon fishers in Eden bow down,
Lift heavy from the loom
A banner with a salmon woven on it—
As the babe from the womb

Wrapped in the electric fleece
Of constellations,
Robed in the rainbow nakedness
Of oceans.

# Daffodils

*From* Birthday Letters, *the sequence of poems Hughes wrote to his wife Sylvia Plath over a period of twenty-five years and only published some months before his death.*


Remember how we picked the daffodils ?
Nobody else remembers, but I remember.
Your daughter came with her armfuls, eager and happy,
Helping the harvest.  She has forgotten.
She cannot even remember you.  And we sold them.
It sounds like sacrilege, but we sold them.
Were we so poor ?  Old Stoneman, the grocer,
Boss-eyed, his blood-pressure purpling to beetroot
(It was his last chance,
He would die in the same great freeze as you),
He persuaded us.  Every Spring
He always bought them, sevenpence a dozen,
"A custom of the house".

Besides, we still weren't sure we wanted to own
Anything.  Mainly we were hungry
To convert everything to profit.
Still nomads—still strangers
To our whole possession.  The daffodils
Were incidental gilding of the deeds,
Treasure trove.  They simply came,
And they kept on coming.
As if not from the sod but falling from heaven.
Our lives were still a raid on our own good luck.

We knew we'd live for ever.  We had not learned
What a fleeting glance of the everlasting
Daffodils are.  Never identified
The nuptial flight of the rarest ephemera—
Our own days !
                    We thought they were a windfall.
Never guessed they were a last blessing.

So we sold them.  We worked at selling them
As if employed on somebody else's
Flower-farm.  You bent at it
In the rain of that April—your last April.
We bent there together, among the soft shrieks
Of their jostled stems, the wet shocks shaken
Of their girlish dance-frocks—
Fresh-opened dragonflies, wet and flimsy,
Opened too early.

We piled their frailty lights on a carpenter's bench,
Distributed leaves among the dozens—
Buckling blade-leaves, limber, groping for air, zinc-
                    silvered—
Propped their raw butts in bucket water.
Their oval, meaty butts,
And sold them, sevenpence a bunch—

Wind-wounds, spasms from the dark earth,
With their odourless metals,
A flamy purification of the deep grave's stony cold
As if ice had a breath—

We sold them, to wither.
The crop thickened faster than we could thin it.
Finally, we were overwhelmed
And we lost our wedding-present scissors.

Every March since they have lifted again
Out of the same bulbs, the same
Baby-cries from the thaw,
Ballerinas too early for music, shiverers
In the draughty wings of the year.
On that same groundswell of memory, fluttering
They return to forget you stooping there
Behind the rainy curtains of a dark April,
Snipping their stems.

But somewhere your scissors remember.  Wherever
                    they are.
Here somewhere, blades wide open,
April by April
Sinking deeper
Through the sod—an anchor, a cross of rust.

# ANDREW MOTION

1952–

It was universally acknowledged when Ted Hughes died that the choice of his successor would be a difficult one. This is nothing new—several times during the 300-year history of the poet laureateship, critics of the post have questioned its relevance, argued for its abolition and publicly challenged the new incumbent. There were regrets when Tennyson, the greatest laureate to date, was preferred to Elizabeth Barrett Browning. After Hughes's death there was much talk of the need for a 'people's poet', for a woman laureate, even for doing away with a post that, in a modern democracy, could be seen as an embarrassing anachronism.

Whoever succeeded Ted Hughes was likely to be pilloried and praised in equal measure. The appointment of Andrew Motion has disappointed the abolitionists and the reformers and greatly pleased his admirers, mindful of his past championing of poetry, both as editor and publisher, and of his work for the arts in general as a member of the Arts Council. He has also published eight collections of verse and a *Selected Poems 1976–1997*, as well as critical studies of Philip Larkin and Edward Thomas, and biographies of the Lamberts, Philip Larkin and John Keats.

In Motion's poetry the personal and the public are closely entwined. His family and the people he loves keep company in his mind with historical and legendary figures. Private dramas, the stories of individual lives broaden into larger narratives. The poet Ruth Padel has written of his search for different ways of "panning out from individual vulnerability to wide-angle shots of the whole human landscape". Yet, no matter how terrible the events described, how strong the sense of pain, the voice in the poems is never forced, rarely raised. In lightly, loosely stressed lyrics and elegies, Motion weaves together past and present, private and public, reliving and observing an experience, fixing and suspending it in time.

Motion has described poetry as something very primitive, a kind of hotline to our deepest feelings and deepest selves. It is, he warns us, inherently subversive, against the grain. It approaches traditional orthodoxies from an oblique angle. He describes himself as a natural reformer, determined to broaden the franchise of the laureateship. He is the first laureate to be appointed for ten years only—time enough to bring about the changes he intends, to speak to an ever changing, increasingly diverse society in a clear, distinctive voice.

# In the Attic

*One of several very moving poems that Andrew Motion has written about his mother, who was badly injured in a riding accident and lay in a coma for some years before she died.*

Even though we know now
your clothes will never
be needed, we keep them,
upstairs in a locked trunk.

Sometimes I kneel there
touching them, trying to relive
time you wore them, to catch
the actual shape of arm and wrist.

My hands push down
between hollow, invisible sleeves,
hesitate, then take hold
and lift :

a green holiday ;  a red christening ;
all your unfinished lives
fading through dark summers
entering my head as dust.

# A Blow to the Head

*First published in the collection* Love in a Life *in 1991.*

On the metro,
two stops in from Charles de Gaulle,
somebody slapped my wife.

Just like that—
a gang of kids—
for moving her bag
from the seat to her lap :
a thunderclap
behind my back.

Very next thing
was reeling dark
and the kids outside
beside themselves :
*You didn't see !  You didn't see !*
*It might be him !  It wasn't me !*

For the rest,
she wept through every station into Paris,
her head on my shoulder like love at the start
of its life.

*

By the merest chance
I had in mind
J. K. Stephen,
who damaged his head
on a visit to Felix-
stowe (Suffolk) in '86.

*The nature of the accident is not certainly known ;
in the Stephen family it was said he was struck
by some projection from a moving train.*

Not a serious blow,
but it drove him mad
(molesting bread
with the point of a sword ;
seized with genius—
painting all night),

and finally killed him
as well as his father,
who two years later
surrendered his heart
with a definite crack
like a sla...

*

...which reminds me.
When I was a kid
a man called Morris
slapped my face
so crazily hard
it opened a room
inside my head
where plates of light
skittered and slid
and wouldn't quite
fit, as they were
meant to, together.

It felt like the way,
when you stand between mirrors,
the slab of your face
shoots backwards and forwards
for ever and ever
with tiny delays,
so if you could only
keep everything still
and look to the end
of the sad succession,
time would run out
and you'd see yourself dead.

\*

There is an attic flat
with views of lead
where moonlight rubs
its greasy cream,

and a serious bed
where my darling wife
lies down at last
and curls asleep.

I fit myself
along her spine
but dare not touch
her breaking skull,

and find my mother
returns to me
as if she was climbing
out of a well :

ginger with bruises,
hair shaved off,
her spongy crown
is ripe with blood.

I cover my face
and remember a dog
in a reeking yard
when the kid I was

came up to talk.
I was holding a choc
in a folded fist,
but the dog couldn't tell

and twitched away—
its snivelling whine
like human fear,
its threadbare head

too crankily sunk
to meet my eye
or see what I meant
by my opening hand.


## On the Table

*A love poem, ostensibly a man's view of a woman's dress, in reality his
gradual laying out of all his emotional cards on the table.*

I would like to make it clear that I have bought
this tablecloth with its simple repeating pattern
of dark purple blooms not named by any botanist
because it reminds me of that printed dress you had
the summer we met—a dress you have always said
I never told you I liked. Well I did, you know. I did.
I liked it a lot, whether you were inside it or not.

How did it slip so quietly out of our life ?
I hate—I really hate—to think of some other bum
swinging those heavy flower-heads left to right.
I hate even more to think of it mouldering on a tip
or torn to shreds—a piece here wiping a dipstick,
a piece there tied round a crack in a lead pipe.

It's all a long time ago now, darling, a long time,
but tonight just like our first night here I am
with my head light in my hands and my glass full,
staring at the big drowsy petals until they start to swim,
loving them but wishing to lift them aside, unbutton them,
tear them, even, if that's what it takes to get through
to the beautiful, moon-white, warm, wanting skin of you.

## Hey Nonny

*First published in* Salt Water, *1997.*

I thought when the glass dropped and did not break
that the world I lived and breathed in was a fake,

and throwing the same glass out through a window
to hear it actually smash on the brick path below

didn't mean : *Oh, that's all right then, everything's OK,*
it meant thinking : *I see. Brilliant. In every possible way*

*this fake is complete and perfect. Look at the stem—*
*a shattered icicle ; look at the brim no longer a brim ;*

*look at those two horny dogs which heard the crash*
*now swivelled apart, heads down and off in a rush.*

*That shows how complete and perfect. Everything just*
*a make-believe of itself. A dream. Nothing on trust.*

Then I swivelled my own head a little. There was the world
caught as my glass had been caught, between held and not-held :

the ash in my garden awake and bristled with spring,
its fistfuls of buds half-showing their soot-coloured wings ;

new moss in the gutter ;   new haze of threadbare grass ;
new crocus clumps plumping ;   new everything filled with the
                    grace

of life between nothing and something, filled with the sense
of learning again to belong, to be quickened by chance,

to be pitched once more through undoubtable air for the sake
of finding what next is in store, to fall, to see if I break.

# Epithalamium
## St. George's Chapel, Windsor

*Andrew Motion's first laureate poem, written for the marriage of Prince
Edward and Sophie Rhys-Jones on 19 June 1999.*

One day, the tissue-light through stained glass falls
on vacant stone, on gaping pews, on air
made up of nothing more than atom storms
which whiten silently, then disappear.

The next, all this is charged with brimming life.
A people-river floods those empty pews,
and music-torrents break—but then stop dead
to let two human voices make their vows :

*to work—so what is true today remains the truth ;*
*to hope—for privacy and what its secrets show ;*
*to trust—that all the world can offer it will give ;*
*to love—and what it has to understand to grow.*

FIRST
PUBLISHED IN 1999
BY ORION MEDIA, AN IMPRINT
OF ORION BOOKS LTD
ORION HOUSE, 5 UPPER ST MARTIN'S LANE,
LONDON WC2H 9EA.

DESIGNED AT CYPHER
12 ST. MARTIN'S COURT, LONDON SE27 0AN

THIS EDITION PRODUCED FOR
THE BOOK PEOPLE LTD
HALLWOOD AVENUE
HAYDOCK, ST HELENS
WA11 9UL

A
CIP CATALOGUE RECORD
FOR THIS BOOK IS
AVAILABLE FROM
THE BRITISH
LIBRARY.

ISBN 0–75281–859–7

PRINTED AND BOUND IN GREAT BRITAIN
BUTLER & TANNER LTD, FROME AND LONDON.